A Death in Jerusalem

Richard Holloway was born in Glasgow in November 1933 and educated locally until he went to Kelham in 1948. He remained there until 1956, although with a break for military service in the army, 1952-3.

After leaving Kelham he served as secretary to the Bishop of Accra, Richard Roseveare, 1956-8, and then completed his theological studies in Edinburgh, London and New York. He was ordained a deacon in September 1959 and a priest in June 1960, serving two parishes in Glasgow until spending a sabbatical year (1967-8) at Union Theological Seminary in New York. His other pastorates have included Old Saint Paul's, Edinburgh (1968-80), the Church of the Advent, Boston (1980-84), and St Mary Magdalen, Oxford (1984-86). He is now the Anglican Bishop of Edinburgh, Scotland.

Bishop Holloway is the author of several books, writes regularly for *The Church Times* and for *The Living Church* (USA), and has conducted missions in England, South Africa, Australia, Canada and various cities of the USA.

Other books by Richard Holloway

Let God Arise
New Vision of Glory
A New Heaven
Beyond Belief
Signs of Glory
The Killing
  (*Winner of the Winifred Mary Stanford prize*)
The Anglican Tradition (*Editor*)
Suffering, Sex, and Other Paradoxes

RICHARD HOLLOWAY

A Death in Jerusalem

With a Foreword by
the Archbishop of Canterbury

MOREHOUSE-BARLOW

First published by Fount Paperbacks, London,
in association with Faith Press, in 1986

Holloway, Richard.
A death in Jerusalem.

1. Jesus Christ—Passion—Meditations. 2. Stations
of the Cross—Meditations. I. Title.
BT431.H65 1986   232.9'6   86-21788
ISBN 0-8192-1392-6

To my Father
and
in memory of
my Mother

Contents

Acknowledgements

The version of scripture used throughout is the Revised Standard Version. I would like to acknowledge the use of copyright material from the following publications: to Mr Martyn Skinner for permission to quote from *The Return of Arthur;* to Atheneum House Inc., for permission to quote from *The Last of the Just;* to Faber and Faber for permission to quote from *Murder in the Cathedral* and *Four Quartets*; to Inter-Varsity Press for "The Cry of Earth's Anguish Went Up Unto God" by C. L. Drawbridge, taken from *The Mystery of Suffering* by Hugh Evans Hopkin; and to Bob Bridges for permission to use his poem *Crux* at the beginning of the volume. I would also like to thank my wife, Jeannie, for patiently typing this book.

Richard Holloway   Oxford, 1985

Foreword

by the Archbishop of Canterbury

In *A Death in Jerusalem* Richard Holloway has given us a fine series of vivid and evocative meditations on seven stations of the cross. The author does not spare us—he leads us along the Via Dolorosa into the misery and mystery of the Passion.

But this book is about more than a death in Jerusalem, two thousand years ago. The events of Good Friday are both unique and typical, local and universal, temporary and permanent. They disclose an inexhaustible treasure of meaning which translates time past into time present.

These imaginative meditations on the Way of the Cross have a sacramental quality. They bring yesterday's characters and events into today, and they show how the killing of Jesus can speak powerfully and movingly to our own time and condition.

Such is the heart of faith—when moments of history are presently experienced and rendered full of significance and promise. I hope this book will be widely and carefully read. It will help transform the folly and scandal of the Crucified into a vision of the living power and wisdom of God.

May 1985

Crux

Trees are tall trawlers: floats of blossom; meshes
of leaves seining the wind; reticulations of twig
sifting the cold crosscurrents of the air all day
for drifting life, and drawing fluff-clad flotsam in,
till every timber tower at bedtime hoards a shoal
of feathered parties, cocking bright eyes, crooning
a dark contented language in the wood's black scantlings.

Forest and orchard, grove, hedge and hangar yield
oil and resin, fruit in season, branch for fire
in time of frost; answer the carpenter with rafter, upright;
accept the white flake's fret, the blossom's burden
and pay the auburn forfeit of the fall. Trees
offer to the needs of men, solace of beauty; use
and shelter; a locus for time's progress round the year.

But this tree, out of time, answers no season; refuses
the drift of spring, the push of bud, the winterflower
of snow; unlike the wood in autumn, does not suffer
the timely fall of the faded leaf. Useless. Unlovely. Only
it bleeds a question—Who
set it, a net in the air, to catch what lives at nightfall?
Or nailed it (black ungainly refuge) to the sky?

Bob Bridges

1
The Way of the Cross

The killing of Jesus is one of the oldest of old stories, but it is vast and depthless in its meaning, and it can be approached on many levels. To the mind of faith it contains a revelation from God that bears and demands endless repetition, that constant pondering of the story and its elements we call meditation. But even to the agnostic mind this death is a pivotal event, and not just because it is a significant event in world history. It is one of those representative deaths that capture and contain some of the permanent elements in the human drama. The killing of Jesus is a paradigm, a basic example or pattern of the tragic conflicts inherent in human life. It has given us a vocabulary, a set of images and a cast of characters that have constant validity. They irresistibly assert themselves in all sorts of ways, in all sorts of situations. They provide us with the classic elements of betrayal, of inarticulate innocence overwhelmed by complex and articulate evil, of cowardice, courage and loss.

One of the classic ways in which Christians have meditated on the death of Jesus has been through a series of meditations on what are called "stations of the cross". The stations depict fourteen incidents in the progress of Jesus from his trial before Pilate to the laying of his dead body in the tomb. The devotion probably arose out of the practice of pilgrims at Jerusalem of following the traditional way of the cross from Pilate's house to Calvary. Most of the incidents depicted are either found in, or are deducible from, the account of the passion found in the gospels. The fourteen incidents represented by the stations are as follows: Christ standing before Pilate is condemned to death, Christ receives his cross; Christ falls for the first time; Christ meets his mother; Simon of Cyrene is made to bear the cross; Christ's face is wiped by Veronica; he falls for the second time; he meets the women of Jerusalem; he falls for the third time; he is stripped of his garments; he is nailed to the cross; Christ dies on the cross; his body is taken down from the cross and laid in the arms of his mother; his body is laid in the tomb.

Painters and woodcarvers have loved to depict these incidents, and they still have a powerful hold on the artistic imagination. Their hold on the Christian imagination is permanent and understandable; for us these are revelatory events, they disclose meaning to us, but the disclosure of meaning is not something easy and immediate. This meaning has to be waited for, often in silence, before it will yield itself to our attention. This assumes, of course, that these are living events with which we can be personally involved. This is quite a difficult thing to describe in theory, though most believers will understand it well from their experience.

There seem to be three ways of experiencing time: there is the past, what we look back to but can no longer experience except in memory and imagination; there is the present, the moving point of time, what we are experiencing now, though it is always slipping into the past; and there is a third way of experiencing time, what we might call the past made sacramentally present. In spiritual history certain events have a unique sacramental identity that gives them a character of permanent presence. The spiritual reality makes itself present to us by providing itself with a historic or material form, by means of which it accompanies us through time. The sacramental mode is adopted for our sake because it is the only language we understand. What is called sacred history has this character. The Christian Year, the endless repetition of the story of Christ and the Church, is much more than a fond remembrance of times past. For those who believe, those who enter into the mystery of the redemption of time, the yearly remembrance of the life of Christ is a way of actualizing and making that life present now, in the universal mode of sacramental reality. To the outsider or the occasional participant, this may not appear to be the case. This is because the meaning of the experience cannot first be found outside the experience as a reason for seeking it. Its meaning is always within, not outside, the experience, and submission has to be made first, consent has to be given in advance.

All of this applies with special force to the story of the killing of Jesus. Here is an event that can be read on many levels. It can be seen as a poignant human story about a brilliant and charismatic outsider who challenged the system and was destroyed by it, and that is certainly a valid way to interpret it. But that interpretation cannot account for every layer of meaning in this event, nor does it really dispose of the mystery that surrounds the cross. The fact is that the cross does not lend itself to any single, simple explanation, and even the sum of all explanations leaves it strangely resistant to understanding. Even Christians who think they know what the cross means have never really agreed among themselves as to its exact interpretation. There is no official Christian doctrine that does for the death of Jesus what the Council of Chalcedon of 451 did in defining the nature of Christ as One Person in Two Natures, human and divine. Christians are convinced of the centrality of the cross, but they have been wisely reluctant to define and delimit its meaning. Definition and delimitation, anyway, can be marks of death, signs that the object or event under consideration is now static, observable, something we can walk round. It is unlikely that any event in history can be absolutely defined in that way, but it is certainly the case that the cross resists that treatment. This is partly because the motives of the main protagonists are shrouded in mystery and are no longer available to our interrogation, but it is mainly because there is something defiantly contemporary about this event. Those who contemplate it steadily and patiently find that it is still living and active, still sacramentally present to them, no longer just an event in the past. They find, in fact, that the stations of the cross are more than pious images on the walls of churches; they can be revelatory symbols, the means through which divine truth is communicated to men and women. There are a number of words in the Christian vocabulary that are used to describe this kind of activity. The most common is revelation, but we also talk about "manifestations" and "epiphanies". The words all convey the sense of something hidden that is now disclosed, something covered or obscure that is made clear. And these revelations are never public spectacles, there is no general disclosure made, it is always private and personal. Meaning comes to individuals, never to multitudes. This is because the thing or person that bears the revelation has to be attended to, waited upon, and can easily be missed. The events that bear the epiphany can be looked upon with such a swift and careless gaze that they are never allowed to offer up their meaning. We become trapped by the narrowness of our seeing and the limits of our knowing.

The experience of revelation raises acutely the most offensive element in Christianity, what C. H. Dodd called "the scandal of particularity". Most people can accept some generalized form of theism. As they might say, "they believe in God". What offends them about Christianity is its assertion that this remote and generalized concept of a distant divinity actually invests itself in particular forms, in particular times and places. There is little point in arguing about it, however. What court on earth could possibly judge the claims of revelation? People are not argued into faith in Christ. When faith comes it is the response to an epiphany, a disclosure, and it is difficult to describe it in prose. Music and poetry capture it best. Let me quote a piece of poetry that seems to capture something of the process of recognition that goes on, as well as providing an insight into the scandal of a God who chooses to invest himself in the particular. It comes from a poem called *The Return of Arthur* by Martyn Skinner. An unbeliever finds himself entranced in a church, gazing at a wooden plaque of the Nativity.

> So Leo gazed, absorbed, a timeless glance;
> And thought of all the trees that nature held
> (Strange instance of a trance within a trance);
> Cedars of Lebanon, green beechwoods delled
> With sapphire; sombre newsprint forests felled
> At such a rate, each Sunday men were able

To read ten acres at the breakfast table;
Dwarf fairy oaks at Lichen, harled with moss;
Trunks wide as roads; through which a cart
   could go;
A jungle mat a continent across
Which, piled as logs, would make the Alps look
   low—
And yet of all that ever grew, or grow
   (So ran his thoughts) this carving had been
      done
Uniquely from a random plank of one.

Was not the contrast much the same in space,
Whose glittering forests were the galaxies?
For if the carver made a special case,
Selecting from innumerable trees
One segment, so from the vast host of these
   Could not the prime Creator, mightier far,
Have carved his story on a single star?

And if he had, Ah, if indeed he had,
And come himself to earth, a newborn cry,
Would not the story have been just like that;
And signs accompanied, in earth and sky,
That holy abdication from on high;
   And radiant beings from about the throne
   Of light, have made the lamplit stable
      known?

Meditating on the stations of the cross can have the same
sort of revelational impact. As we contemplate the cross
we will learn much about human nature. More impor-
tantly, we will learn about God's way with human nature.

2
Christ Before Pilate

The first station is the condemnation of Christ before Pilate. A skilled artist can capture the essence of the incident in a few lines of a pen or strokes of a brush. We see the silent Christ, the crown of thorns on his head, his body bloodied by the recent whipping, standing before Pontius Pilate, Governor of Judea, sitting on the judgement seat, having just passed sentence of death. Behind this simple and touching scene lie complex issues.

Before we actually turn to Pilate and seek to understand him, we have to ask about the religious leaders of Jerusalem, "the chief priests, with the elders and scribes", who had arrested Jesus and brought him bound to Pilate. Why did they conspire to put Jesus to death? The only motive that is attributed to them is envy. Mark, followed by Matthew, tells us that Pilate sought to release Jesus because "he perceived that it was out of envy that the chief priests had delivered him up" (Mark 15:10). Envy has always been a characteristic sin of the priest, as well as of the artist, perhaps because priests and artists deal in commodities that are difficult to measure exactly, with the result that they depend upon the approval of others for their validation. Inevitably, they feel threatened by the popularity of rivals, and the sin of envy grows in them.

Envy is often confused with jealousy, but there is an important distinction to be made between them. The

7

jealous man wants to *possess* his neighbour's goods. In the words of the tenth commandment, he wants to possess his neighbour's house, or his neighbour's wife, or his servant, or his maid, or his ox, or his ass. Jealousy is a positive sin: it is a craving, gnawing desire for something you do not possess. Envy, on the other hand, is not a positive sin, it is entirely negative. The envious man *regrets* his neighbour's fortune, he grieves secretly over his neighbour's luck. Envy has been defined as "sorrow for another's good", but it can also take the form of secret satisfaction at the misfortune of your friend. In fact, envy is frequently found among friends, it is a sin among equals, and its most dominant characteristic is negative. It offers no pleasure, no satisfaction. Every other sin offers some gratification, at least for a time, but envy offers little—it is an empty and desolating experience from beginning to end.

When it takes over a person it produces certain obvious symptoms, the most conspicuous of which is malice. Envious people have a peculiar gift for chipping away at the reputation of others, praising them in one breath and damning them with some qualifying phrase in the next. The envious have a special facility for noting the defects of others. Another characteristic of the envious person is hypocrisy. Envy is a sin among equals and friends, so it strikes in those relations where love is supposed to rule. When a man hears of the good fortune of a friend or equal he can speak one thing but feel another. He expresses delight, but he has to draw it up from a well of bitterness. Yet another characteristic of envy is dejection. Envy is sorrow for another's good; it can be depressing to witness the blessing or popularity of another, especially if you know the person well. Jesus never spoke a truer word than when he said that a prophet is not without honour, save in his own country and among his own friends and relations.

There can be no doubt that Jesus provoked envy both among his relatives and acquaintances and among the religious leaders of his people. We hear the envious muttering in the background of the gospels as he makes his mark. "Isn't this Joseph's son? Who does he think he is?" "Our credentials as leaders of the faith of our fathers are impeccable, but where does this illegitimate upstart get the authority to teach?" We know that the common people heard him gladly because he spoke with freshness, with the authority of personal experience and "not as the scribes", who had fallen into the trap that confronts the professional religious teacher in every age: the reduction of deeply felt human experience of God to a formula that is then applied narrowly and unimaginatively to every situation. This formalizing of human experience into law is a basic temptation in every area of life, and at its root lies a fear of freedom, and its insecurity and vulnerability.

It was the very freedom of Jesus that alarmed the religious leaders of his day, but we must be careful in defining and understanding that freedom, for even freedom can be formalized into anarchy and become, in turn, an abstraction. Jesus was felt to be threatening his contemporaries because there was no hidden agenda in his relations with God and with men and women. Most of us are really only interested in ourselves, and even our love for God and friends can become a mode or expression or vehicle of that egotism. Sociologists call this phenomenon "instrumentalization": the person, whether God or a fellow human being, is used by us in some way to further our own projects. This is seen most clearly among religious professionals. The whole object of religion is the celebration of God and the discovery of his will for our lives. Inevitably, round that central purpose has accrued a whole series of structures that were originally meant to aid and express it, but which have become ends in themselves. Religion, in fact, can become simply another way of expressing human egotism. It can become a career that offers rewards and ways of measuring success that have only a very tenuous connection with its true end, which is the glory of God. The ecclesiastical novels of Anthony Trollope capture this very well, in a rather innocent way. They are all about the politics of the cathedral close, the human and superficial side of ecclesiastical life, with the same human dynamics as are found in the political novels. In Barchester one seeks a canonry or a good living or a bishopric; in Westminster one works to become secretary to some rising star or one conspires to win a seat in the cabinet. The clothes and the vocabulary are different, but it is the same game, the same old human game of satisfying the self.

But even if we avoid such a blatant instrumentalization of religion, there are subtle variants that are more difficult to miss. The object of religion is the knowledge of God, but God is elusive to our senses and we have to fall back on secondary realities in order to express something of his nature and reality. Words are an obvious example. We use words to express and define what we think we know about God, but it is obvious that the words are not God, though something of his reality comes through them. However, it is a simple and almost unavoidable step to accord the words, the formulas about God, an almost Godlike status. We are in a terrible dilemma here:

we cannot know God as he is in himself, but only as he has revealed himself through intermediate realities, such as words or experiences in history. The words or experiences are guides, valuable and essential for the wise pilgrim, but they are not the object of the pilgrimage. The difference between them and God is much like the difference between an ordnance survey map of a mountain and the mountain itself. The map is a necessary part of the equipment of the wise climber, but only an obsessive cartographer would argue that it is a substitute for the mountain. Unfortunately, professional religious guides can easily fall into the trap of the obsessive cartographer. Instead of helping men and women to experience God, to climb the mountain, they can baffle them with map references and climber's jargon, and they can assume proprietorship over the mountain by refusing to admit uncertified guides. Something like this seems to have happened between Jesus and the religious leaders of his day. He spoke about God in a way that showed there was no third element involved, no intermediate formula, no map. He spoke, we are told, "as one having authority", as one who knew the mountain intimately and as one who was not afraid to contradict the local guides who earned their living from the mountain, but who had become obsessed with the secondary industries that had grown up round it. The same thing can happen to any institution. Peter Berger describes the process as bureaucratization, and says that for the bureaucrat the ideal institution is one with no clients—a hospital with no patients, a school with no students, a welfare agency with no poor people inconveniently interrupting its smooth efficiency.

So the envy the religious leaders of Jerusalem felt as

they observed the impact Jesus was making naturally shaded into something stronger. His sheer popularity must have galled them and threatened their authority, but it was the substance of his teaching that finally outraged them and goaded them into action. In all the accounts of the trial of Jesus it is obvious that the real accusation levelled against him was blasphemy, and that the root of the accusation lay in the authoritative way Jesus spoke about God, interpreted God's law and extended God's forgiveness. In short, he did not behave like a human intermediary who interprets the tradition about God, or, to revert to an earlier metaphor, offers guidance in using the maps provided for the human pilgrimage to God. The gravamen of the charge against him was that he spoke not *about* God but *as* God, as the one sent from God. I do not think we can doubt the sincerity of their accusation. As strict monotheists they had no alternative but to charge him with a particularly gross form of blasphemy. We can also be fairly certain that their righteous anger must have been agreeably heightened by the envy that lurked beneath the surface. The only pleasure that envy ever affords is to witness the downfall of one greater than yourself. Envy is very good at covering its traces, so it is probable that the enemies of Jesus never acknowledged their own motives. After all, what further witnesses did they need, having heard the blasphemy with their own ears? His claims were preposterous and, according to the fierce standards of the day, deserved death unless they were true, a possibility that never for a moment seemed to occur to them. He deserved to die, but as only the Governor could pronounce sentence of death, they brought Jesus to Pilate.

The gospels only give us a few paragraphs to describe the meeting between Jesus and Pilate, but they offer all the elements for a perceptive sketch of the Roman Governor, delineate certain permanent characteristics of the conflict between politics and spirituality, and in a few swift strokes capture Pilate's ambivalence and harsh complexity. It is immediately obvious to him that Jesus is not a criminal, and that any offence he has committed does not belong in his own jurisdiction, but is presumably some obscure matter related to the tiresome superstitions of the Jews, who pursued their religious beliefs with baffling and wearying intensity, making the administration of Judea both complex and unpredictable. Pilate has no appetite for the drama that is unfolding before him, and casts about for an escape. He hopes the mob will provide him with the escape hatch he needs, and appeals to them over the heads of their leaders.

Pilate was a shrewd administrator, he must have known something about the reputation of Jesus, and have penetrated to the motive behind the outrage of the priests. Why not set the mob to decide between the charismatic preacher who had attracted such a following and that pompous cabal at the Temple? Crowds are volatile things, however, and they are usually for rent to the highest bidder, no matter whether the form of exchange is silver, the glow of self-righteousness or the sight of blood. As all the world now knows, the crowd called for Barabbas, so Pilate still had Jesus on his hands. Luke tells us that Pilate tried to palm him off on Herod, but that astute princeling soon sent him back to the Governor.

The whole episode is instructive. It is hard to tell whether Pilate is motivated by distaste for the obvious machinations of the priests or by some residual sense of justice. What seems to be clear, however, is that he was endowed with a large share of political prudence. Politicians obviously enjoy it when the path of virtue and the path of expedience coincide, for then they can parade their conscience. It is much more difficult for them when the paths diverge and they have to make a choice. Pilate's dilemma seems to be straightforward. He probably viewed Jesus with the sort of puzzled condescension that often characterizes the attitude of those in power towards the saintly. The powerful usually recognize power in others, even when it is spiritual power, but powerful politicians, used to trading in compromise and expedience, are often impatient with single-minded saints who seem not to care about the consequences of their actions. Pilate paid Jesus the compliment of giving him some attention, but it was a busy man's attention, perfunctory and half-mocking. He knew the dilemma he faced, probably sensed the direction he would take. Jesus would add nothing to, or subtract nothing from, his problem. That Jesus was innocent was obvious, but it was just as obvious that releasing him would be politically dangerous. The mob was inflamed and the Temple leaders were a manipulative bunch with whom he had to go on living. Pilate finally gives in to them, but he claims the impotent man's revenge with an elaborately sarcastic joke. He dresses Jesus up like a pantomime king and brings him forth: "Behold your king!" "We have no king but Caesar", they scream in blasphemous fury. That was the irony Pilate had fished for, but it can't have been much consolation to him as he turned and tramped back into the palace, while Jesus was swallowed up by the mob below.

What did Jesus make of Pilate? According to John's gospel Jesus addressed Pilate in a way that will bear considerable meditation: "You would have no power over me unless it had been given you from above; therefore he who delivered me to you has the greater sin" (John 19:11). We can deduce several things from this immediately, while some other insights will require a little more digging.

In the first place it is obvious that Jesus recognized that what Pilate was having to do was sinful, though his sin was smaller than that of the religious leaders who had contrived the whole incident. Sin there was, but there is a suggestion that Jesus recognized that it was an inescapable part of the dilemma of power in which Pilate found himself. People in authority are called upon every day to make hard decisions between competing goods and between inescapable evils, and the calculus of power rarely affords them a perfect choice. One can almost see Pilate figuring the odds as he strides between Jesus and the priests who stood outside: to give them their way with Jesus will be an obvious miscarriage of justice involving the death of an innocent man; to refuse them their way will lead to a riot, with hundreds killed in Jerusalem and much displeasure felt in Rome. Only a childlike innocence pursues right without regard to consequences, and those who win power in this world usually abandon their innocence at an early stage in their struggle.

The dilemmas of power, the agony of hard choices, create enormous problems for Christians, and many of them, knowing little about the realities of political conflict, are prone to give soft answers and seek for sentimental solutions. Jesus does not seem to have done that. He rarely spoke on the subject, and when he did, as in the celebrated command to give God and Caesar their appropriate tributes, his remarks were hardly straightforward. To resort to theological language, we could say that Jesus recognized that all political institutions, indeed all human institutions, were "fallen", because they reflected human nature. There is a mysteriously intractable element in human affairs that resists the application of love and goodness, and it is writ large in groups and nations. Jesus tacitly recognized the flawed nature of human institutions by his submission to Pilate, by his acceptance of the necessities that beset the haughty Roman Governor. But there is an important sense in which it is Pilate who stands under the authority of Jesus. At no time do we get from Jesus any feeling of abjection, of being swept along by forces beyond his control. His submission is a voluntary abdication of power, an act of self-limitation. Later in this book we must try to explore the difference between that and suicide, and we must try to understand the meaning of this death. Meanwhile it is something to recognize that Jesus acknowledged, and to some extent validated, the choice Pilate made. At any rate, his most sweeping condemnation was reserved for the spiritual leaders who had forced the dilemma on Pilate. The most straightforward way to understand their "greater sin" is as a plot to encompass the judicial murder of a man innocent of any political crime. The priests not only plotted to kill Jesus, they arranged it so that the State would have to do their dirty work for them. That is blatant and straightforward evil, but we probably ought to detect an even more fateful element behind the crime. The relationship between spiritual and secular institutions, between Church and State, is highly problematic, and the perfect balance is rarely achieved. Spiritual institutions have, at one time or another, developed every conceivable type of response to the reality of the secular order, but there are certain basic trends that are worth noting.

There has often been a temptation for the spiritual authority in a nation to recruit the secular or temporal power to do its bidding. In the case of established churches, for instance, this has often involved limitations and penalties imposed upon nonconforming religious bodies. This is by no means confined to the Christian world. It is, for instance, a dominant characteristic of Islamic culture. Wherever and however it appears, it inevitably leads to the corruption of the religion that is in power. But this is a pattern that is no longer officially found in the West today, though there are a number of areas where a considerable residuum from previous eras still complicates religious life. The other tendency is for the spiritual authority to validate and sanctify the secular order by providing it with moral and theological justification. And this is not simply a matter of supporting a government or a party in power, though that can be and frequently is done. A more insidious and pervasive form of this temptation is the way theologians and spiritual leaders allow themselves to be recruited by the prevailing political and intellectual fashions and ideologies. The paradox is, of course, that there are usually several of these going at the same time, all with enthusiastic supporters on the spiritual terraces, all supporting different teams, all shouting each other down.

There seems to be no obvious way through this quagmire, and most of the issues that obsess us are only seen in true perspective when time has moved on and we have the benefit of hindsight. It would seem obvious, however, that Christians should be extremely reluctant to offer their absolute benediction to any political formula, remembering T. S. Eliot's conviction that there is nothing very conclusive about the art of temporal government. Christians should not run the risk of mixing up eternal certainties with temporal expedients. That does not mean, however, that they should not involve themselves in political action and debate. They do anyway, but they should always remember the provisional and uncertain nature of what they do, thereby adding a welcome tinge of modesty to their views. The dignity and silence of Jesus before Pilate would suggest that he recognized the inescapable complexity and muddle of political life, but his reserve on the subject of politicians combined with his stern judgement on ecclesiastics who use the political arm for their own ends, should teach us to be wary of bringing God to mockery by yoking him to some temporal cause.

Questions for Discussion

1. Discuss the sin of envy and try to identify some of its current manifestations.

2. What are the dangers of language about God and how can we offset them?

3. Discuss the dilemmas of temporal power and some of the Church's responses to it.

3
Christ Takes Up the Cross

Pilate's last gesture before submitting to the pressure of the religious leaders of Jerusalem was almost childish in its sarcastic defiance. To annoy the priests and elders he had a board made to hang on the cross of Jesus. Normally criminals carried these placards round their necks as they made their way to the place of execution. The name of the offender and his offence scrawled on the board would be a dreadful warning to the crowds who always turned out on these occasions. In this case, however, Pilate played a little game with the accusers of Christ. On the board he had written: JESUS NAZARENUS REX JUDAEORUM, not only in official Latin but also in Greek and Hebrew: JESUS OF NAZARETH, KING OF THE JEWS. The joke would not have been lost on the people of Jerusalem. They probably relished the irony of the title that hung above the head of the crucified preacher from Nazareth. The cross was a strange parody of a kingly throne, and the crown of thorns was cruelly comic in its effect. The sight of this pantomime king dragging his cross through Jerusalem must have been irresistibly laughable to the coarser elements of the city. Real kings, after all, keep their distance, because it is distance that preserves the mystery that is part of the royal stock-in-trade.

There is certainly a mystery or mysticism that surrounds earthly kings, an awe and glamour that separates them from ordinary mortals. "There's a divinity doth hedge a king", according to Shakespeare. In reality, of course, it is all just expert public relations or personnel management. Power always cloaks itself in impressive garments and sublime language, but there is really no mystery about the origin of kings or chiefs or sheikhs or caliphs. They won their position by might and intelligence and the superior use of force. Away back down the ages, behind every gorgeous succession of powdered monarchs, there lurks a belching and muscular bandit chief who exterminated the opposition and secured his own place. St Augustine illustrates this by telling the story of the pirate who, having been seized by Alexander the Great and asked what he meant by taking possession of the sea, replied: "What do you mean by seizing the whole earth? Because I do it with a petty ship I am called a robber, but you who do it with a great fleet are called an Emperor."

Kings were originally powerful men who kept their authority by force. In the beginning power of this sort was usually very localized in one man, or in one or two. The history of politics is the history of the widening of that power to include more and more people, and that widening or spreading of power has rarely been granted graciously or willingly. In the history of politics power is always won by some sort of pressure, either of violence or of public opinion, or an astute mixture of both. Kings held out against barons; and then king and barons held out against new centres of power; and the new centres of power, of commerce and commons, held out against the widening of that power to include all men; finally, men held out against women, who were only included in the political structures within living memory. And even in the liberal democracies of the West today power is not evenly spread. There are still, and always will be, power blocs and interest groups who hold on to their power and use it to get a better deal for their colleagues, even if it comes at the expense of others. In human history people do not relinquish power willingly: they hold on to it as long as they can, and use it to guard their own way of life.

There are only two ways of dealing with challenges to existing centres of power. The wise way is to share power, however grudgingly, while retaining as much of it for yourself as you can; the other way is to fight to hold on to power against all who challenge it, and that usually ends in a man more powerful than yourself taking over. The point to grasp is that in the world power is king and most people want some share in it with others, or want to wield it over others. There are, of course, always a few in any generation who try to exert pressure on others to include more and more people in the sharing and exercising of power, but history teaches the rather melancholy lesson that power is usually taken, rarely freely given, no matter how subtle or non-violent the pressure towards change might be. The reason behind the enthronement of power is our fear and selfishness: we want the best for ourselves and those who belong to us; others are perceived as a threat to that stability, so we seek to protect our own interests by using power against others. In human history power rules, power is king.

That is why the irony of the cross haunts human history. It is the utter reversal of the way of the world. It is the absolute abnegation of power by one who had access to absolute power. John tells us that Jesus answered Pilate's half-curious, half-mocking question about his kingship in this way: "My kingship is not of this world; if my kingship were of this world, my servants would fight, that I might not be handed over to the Jews; but my kingship is not from the world" (John 18:36). In the first chapter I claimed that, for those with eyes to see, the pattern of the killing of Jesus had revelatory power. The passion of Christ is a manifestation of the nature and activity of God, but it is bewilderingly difficult for us to grasp. All our models of power and authority are useless when it comes to understanding the power of God, except by way of complete reversal. The second station confronts us with the mystery of the cross as a disclosure of the manner of God's dealings with the world. The picture we have of the kingship of Christ in the gospels is a heart-breaking cartoon. We do not see him leading armies or holding forth to great assemblies or receiving the homage of princes. We see him torn, bloody and helpless, nailed to a cross. We see him so helpless he cannot brush away the flies that cling to his wounds or wipe away the blood that runs down his face. There can be no greater helplessness than the experience of hanging on a cross. The last royal portrait of Christ on earth is a picture of abject and total powerless-ness, and above it there hangs the ironic caption penned by the cynical Pilate: JESUS NAZARENUS REX JUDAEORUM. Powerlessness is the message of the cross, the meaning of the second station. The cross is a sign or emblem of God's way with the world.

John puts it another way when he describes part of the encounter between Jesus and Pilate as a dispute about truth or reality: " 'For this I was born, and for this I have come into the world, to bear witness to the truth. Every one who is of the truth hears my voice.' Pilate said to him, 'What is truth?' " (John 18:37-38). Earlier in his gospel John had described Jesus as the truth: "I am the way, and the truth, and the life" (John 14:6). But how can a man be "the truth"? We are back at that mysterious cluster of words: revelation, epiphany, manifestation; in Jesus there is a disclosure of the meaning and nature of God; what we could not find out for ourselves, God disclosed to us in Christ. He is the truth about God, and we see that truth at its most harrowing and unacceptable in the cross. The cross is also the truth of God, it shows the manner of the exercise of the power of God. It shows that God reigns by love, not by power. His authority is exercised by the power of his beseeching and by nothing else: "Is it nothing to you, all you who pass by? Look and see if there is any sorrow like my sorrow . . ." (Lamentations 1:12). God does not grudge every invasion of his rights, does not keep to himself the majesty of his being in a frozen eternity, but pours it out in the creation of the world, and that constant self-offering is still the truth about God. In God's revelation in the cross we see the complete reversal of the world's destructive and selfish use of power. In the book of Revelation there is a mysterious description of Christ as "the Lamb that was slain from the foundation of the world" (Revelation 13:8). What could be more defenceless and less threatening than a lamb? It is the complete opposite of the grasping and fearful man of power. Again, it is an image of reversal, a metaphor that completely contradicts the way of the world. Jesus himself made it quite specific when he said to his disciples: "You know that the rulers of the Gentiles lord it over them, and their great men exercise authority over them. It shall not be so among you; but whoever would be great among you must be your servant, and whoever would be first among you must be your slave; even as the Son of man came not to be served but to serve, and to give his life as a ransom for many" (Matthew 20:25-27).

"It shall not be so among you", he said to the young Church. It was a difficult admonition to heed, and the Church did not take long to find out how impossible it was. Some historians even put a date on it. One afternoon in the year 312 the Emperor Constantine had a vision. He was about to face his rival, Maxentius, in battle for the leadership of the Roman Empire. Constantine was not a Christian, but he strongly disapproved of the persecution of the Christian Church and, being a shrewd politician, he probably saw that it, more than any other agency, could help restore unity to the torn and divided Empire. Whatever his motives, and they were always rather obscure, he told the historian Eusebius that on the afternoon before his final battle with Maxentius he had a vision. He saw a cross of light in heaven bearing the inscription, *In hoc signo vinces,* "You shall conquer by this sign". And during the night while he slept he saw the sign with the same inscription in a dream. So he had a standard made: a spear overlaid with gold, on which a cross was formed by a transverse bar, with a wreath of gold and precious stones enclosing the monogram *Chi* and *Rho* for the name of Christ. On the following after-noon he led his army into battle against Maxentius at the Milvian Bridge. Under the sign of the cross he enthusi-astically massacred his opponents and was soon the senior leader of the Roman Empire. He went on to make Christianity the official religion of the Empire.

Constantine started a trend. Since his day many

Christians have gone into battle under the cross, and destroyed their enemies in the name of the crucified. Perhaps the most celebrated example of this bloodthirsty phenomenon was the crusading movement in the Middle Ages. For three centuries waves of Christian warriors descended upon the Holy Land to slaughter Mohammendans and try to win back the Holy Land for the Church. They were called crusaders because they bore the sign of the cross upon their clothing. One way and another the trend has continued. When they were not slaying Mohammedans or Jews in the name of the crucified, Christians have usually turned upon one another. You could, with justice, write in blood the history of the movement started by Jesus, and as an emblem there is always the cross: By this sign conquer! A great Jewish novelist, meditating on the age-old persecution of Jews by Christians, put these words into the mouth of one of his characters: " 'The Christians say they love Christ, but I think they hate him without knowing it; so they take the cross by the other end and make a sword out of it and strike us with it! You understand, Golda,' he cried suddenly, strangely excited, 'they take the cross and turn it around, they turn it around, my God' " (Andre Schwartz-Bart, *The Last of the Just*). Christians turn the cross around. That's what Constantine did. He turned it around, turned it into a sword. That is what the crusaders did. That is what the Christian Church has always done, one way or another: we take the cross and turn it around so that the instrument of the world's salvation, the sign of the self-emptying of God, becomes yet another weapon in the armoury of power.

Constantine was the most blatant and naive offender in this respect, but there have been others, and those who have literally taken up the sword in the name of Christ are by no means the worst. It is the reversal of the principle of the cross that is important, and the more subtle the reversal the more profound it is. The cross shows us that God's way is not the way of power and control. He conquers only by the power of his beseeching, never by the sheer organization of power. Warriors may have profoundly misunderstood the cross, but they have at least shown a disregard for their own lives that has something Christlike in it. The politicization of the cross is a much grosser type of betrayal, and it has characterized the Church at all times and in all places, not least today. This way of turning the cross around uses the Church, whether at national or local level, as an arena for the exercise of power. It is seen at its most obvious at parish level where people, usually for complex and often unconscious personal reasons, use the local congregation as a way of exercising power, or capturing territory that they guard with absolute single-mindedness. People who behave thus are often ineffective or powerless in other spheres, so they use the Church as a way of compensating for their failure; through the Church they get back at the forces that have robbed them of significance. Almost anything in congregational life can provide an arena for these struggles. It seems that any group, if it is determined enough, can learn how to control or modify any organization and use it for its own ends. It happens in political parties and it happens in the Church. But these little local squabbles are as nothing compared to what happens when the Church's whole constitution is politicized in this way, so that the corporate life of the Church becomes an arena for struggles between competing powers. Many of the churches have done this quite intentionally. They have organized themselves on the parliamentary model, with fateful results. Parliaments are wise and realistic ways of dealing with the fact of competing power structures in society. They are premised, not upon the abnegation of power, but upon the struggle for power. Using the adversative system of the courts, they struggle to achieve a balance of power between competing interests that will enable social systems to function. "But it shall not be so among you," said Christ through the Church, "your way of dealing with the issues of power and control will be by way of self-abnegation and self-effacement. And you have a model in the redemptive strategy of God, the source and creator of all power, who when he took it upon himself to deliver man laid aside his divine nature and took the form of a slave, and being found in fashion as a man, he humbled himself and became obedient unto death, even death on a cross."

Yet who can blame us for resisting the divine strategy of the cross? Even if we can find the courage to take Up the Cross, how can we avoid dismay at the consequences of actions that may lead to the triumph of evil? The death of Christ was the triumph of evil over goodness, and the way of the cross would always appear to guarantee that result, and here it is important to come to grips with the most radical characteristic of the cross. It was not a non-violent tactic in a power struggle between good and evil, a device to change hearts and minds without resort to violence. There are many ways of achieving change and resisting aggression, but they all involve the use of power, whether military or moral. It is often pointed out that Gandhi won a victory over the British Raj by his campaign of non-violent resistance. The issue and consequences of that campaign are irrelevant to the point at issue, which is the claim that Gandhi was following the strategy of Christ. It has to be pointed out that Gandhi's methods, though they may have prevented or minimized bloodshed, were a masterly exercise in the use of power, non-violent power, but still power. There was a clear end in view: the transfer of power from British to Indian rulers. That end was achieved, India won its independence. The argument surrounding non-violent resistance is whether it is a less costly method of countering aggression than resort to violence, and the answer to that question will greatly depend upon the nature of the enemy being resisted. That is an interesting debate, but it really has little to do with the cross of Christ. Christ's death was not an act of non-violent resistance, it was an act of complete non-resistance. It was not a tactic aimed at re-arranging the balance of moral and political power, it was a complete renunciation of power. It has nothing to teach us about dealing with the enormous difficulties we face in handling disputes between individuals, groups and nations, because it is operating on a completely different level of reality. The cross does not answer our questions about the problems that beset us and with which we must deal, usually inefficiently and as we cope with other matters. It is really no use asking questions of the cross or seeking ways to apply its wisdom to our confusions. We are meant, rather, to listen to the cross, to contemplate it so long that something of its divine absurdity begins to penetrate our consciousness so that we begin, at last, to see what God is doing for us through it, rather than endlessly searching for a way of doing something with it for ourselves.

We have to be brought to a point of bafflement by the

cross, maybe even a point of outrage at the moral
absurdity of it, because it is a complete reversal of the
world's standards, including the world's best standards.
The cross turns the world's values around, reverses them,
contradicts them. In the world as it unavoidably comes
to us we protect ourselves by persuasion, then by
pressure; by coercion, then by violence. And the pressure
and the violence can take many forms. Our natural
instinct, when it is unmodified by standards of love,
honour and service (and it is only ever *modified* by these,
it is never totally transformed), is to go for our own
interests, to get our own way, either by manipulation or
confrontation. The pull of the self is always paramount,
however subtle its expression. The way of the self is the
way of the sword, the way of the cross turned around,
the way of assertion, the way one will impose itself on
another.

All of this is profoundly, radically built into our nature,
so it is a matter of no surprise that we do not begin to
understand what God means by the cross. Certainly, St
Peter and the other disciples did not understand it, and
they were closer to it all than we can possibly be. At the
centre of Mark's gospel there is a pivotal moment. Peter
has just blurted out in a second of astonished clarity:
"You are the Christ, the one from God." When Jesus goes
on to explain the strange manner of the kingship that
Peter has only just acknowledged, he is rebuked by Peter.
Peter, like the rest of us, has his own ideas on the subject.
He had looked forward to following a conventional
messiah, a worldly messiah, who would set up a kingdom
in which he, Peter, would have an important position and
where there would be joy and peace and some agreeable
vengeance upon ancient enemies. To his horror Christ

tells him that the Son of man must suffer. We are so used to hearing these words that we think we know what they mean, but I am increasingly persuaded that we do not understand them at all, because to understand them would be in some sense to follow the same way, a way that terrifies and scandalizes us, because it is the way of weakness. It is the weakness of God we see on the cross, the weakness of God that reverses and contradicts the strength of the world.

As we set out on the way of the cross, therefore, we ought to begin by recognizing that the cross does not make sense by any of the standards of logic that we know. But we must resist imposing a meaning upon it, waiting, instead, to see whether its meaning will be disclosed to us. The temptation will be to use the cross, to make it mean what we want it to mean, to turn it around and use it against our enemies. We all end up doing that anyway, but once in a while we should renounce the temptation, and simply follow the cross and seek to discover its own logic. If we do that we may find in the cross, not an echo of our own voice, but the wisdom and power of God.

Questions for Discussion

1. How should power be shared? Discuss some contemporary examples in Church and State.

2. What does the cross teach us about Christ's attitude to power?

3. Has the Church ever applied the logic of the cross in its own use of power?

4
Christ Falls

One of the most defiantly enduring elements in the tradition about Jesus is his sinlessness. Writing to the Corinthians, Paul said that God "for our sake made him to be sin who knew no sin, so that in him we might become the righteousness of God" (2 Corinthians 5:21). The same conviction is reflected in an interestingly oblique way in Matthew's gospel, where Jesus comes to be baptized by John. We read, "John would have prevented him, saying, 'I need to be baptized by you, and do you come to me?' But Jesus answered him, 'Let it be so now; for thus it is fitting for us to fulfil all righteousness'" (Matthew 3:14f). Mark records the baptism of Jesus without comment. Matthew's more elaborate account may be an attempt to get over the difficulty the early Church felt in explaining the meaning of the baptism of Jesus for the remission of sins. Even radical New Testament critics, who operate with a very stringent criterion of historical authenticity, accept the baptism of Jesus, precisely *because* it was an embarrassment to the early Church. The evangelists record it faithfully, even though it puzzled them, and it puzzled them because they were convinced of the sinlessness of Jesus. Perhaps the most eloquent statement of this belief is found in the letter to the Hebrews: "For we have not a high priest who is unable to sympathize with our weaknesses, but one who in every respect has been tempted as we are, yet without sin" (Hebrews 4:15).

Almost every claim the Church has made about Jesus has been assailed or radically re-interpreted at some time or other, but there has been no serious attempt to impugn his sinlessness. Even if Jesus is no longer believed by some to be "perfect God", in the language of the Athanasian Creed, most people still think of him as "perfect man". Of course, a few fantasists have exercised their imaginations on the subject, and over the years there has been a trickle of books claiming that Jesus got down from the cross and ran away to India with Mary Magdalen, but for the most part the tradition of his sinlessness has remained unassaulted.

Jesus is a mystery upon whom we have projected many of our own motives and ideas, but he is strangely resistant to the projection of our sins. We know he was angry often, but there seems to have been a clearness and purity to his anger that purges it of egotism. It was not the anger of the man who is constantly reacting against unresolved tensions in his own nature, blindly hitting out against people who have become accidental symbols of his own hatreds and fears. One feels an uncluttered directness in Jesus, an absence of the invisible third party who usually complicates all human relationships. Most of us bring to our relationships a burden of past rejections and successes, failures and triumphs, that colour and influence the way we are with other people. None of us is pure and straightforward, able to relate to others with absolute unself-consciousness. Unlike the rest of us, however, Jesus did not get in his own way when he was dealing with people. Most people play games with others, power games, posing games, sexual games, games designed to

win their attention and approval. Occasionally we will
find a friend with whom we can be absolutely and truly
ourselves, with no pretence, no fraudulence. Even then,
however, we are rarely ever able to get off the hook of
our own selfhood. It defines us, after all, and definition
is limitation, the setting of boundaries and frontiers, the
narrowing of a thing to itself. Most human conflict is the
almost accidental collision of all these defensive and
isolated little selves, peering out at others from behind
their facades and fortifications. Jesus was without any
of that. There was mystery about him, but it was the
mystery of simplicity, not the mystery of complexity, and
complicated people find it hard to accept simplicity when
they meet it.

I have already discussed the envy that Jesus generated
in the religious leaders of Israel. This again related to
his simplicity. He seems to have lived a life of absolute
poverty. He had no place to lay his head, though he was
clearly welcome in the homes of friends. He had no wife,
though he had many devoted friends, women as well as
men. He depended upon the alms of others for the supply
of necessities during the period of his ministry. In short,
he lived a life of absolute authenticity in which his style
of life and outward conduct exactly reflected and represented his message of absolute trust in God. This kind
of authenticity is rare if not unique, and where it is found
in individuals of spiritual genius it is always a threat to
the official guardians of the message, who rarely practise
what they preach. It is true that his opponents called him
"a wine-bibber and a sinner", but this accusation, from
such a quarter, only enhances the character of Jesus. It
shows us that his sinlessness was not a defect, not a
result of an instinctive nature that had been stunted and

shrivelled by fear or neurosis. His sensual nature was not ruthlessly and unlovingly repressed, resulting in the harsh personality of the puritan for whom life is a constant battle against the lower vices, while daily consenting to "the higher vices, which have to be paid for at higher prices". Jesus imparts nothing of the chilliness of the puritan. In Paul's words, he knew how to be in plenty and how to be in want. The secret of healthy self-denial is to affirm the value of what you deny, not turn it into an object of contempt. This is what Charles Williams called "the way of affirmation of images", and it was the way of Jesus. He loved women and was remarkably free in his dealings with them, in a day when their status was depressed, yet he never married, and there is no tinge of scandal attached to his name. He clearly loved children and they him, often a sign of the straightforward personality. And he obviously appreciated the joy and abundance of nature, without being held in bondage to it. These are the marks of a united personality, in harmony with itself, with no part dangerously repressed, but with every part consenting to be controlled by the authority of the will that gives direction and purpose to life.

From what we can deduce from the tradition, therefore, we derive a picture of Jesus in which his perfection is marked not only by an absence of sin, but by a positive harmony or integration of personality. His sinlessness is not the result of sensual deprivation. It is the consequence of self-transcendence.

But an equally enduring part of the tradition about Jesus is that, like us, he knew temptation. The letter to the Hebrews tells us that he was "touched with our infirmities" and "tempted as we are, yet without sin".

Matthew, Mark and Luke all give an account of the temptation of Jesus in the wilderness, with Matthew and Luke filling out the bald statement in Mark that "he was in the wilderness forty days, tempted by Satan". Paul, as we have seen, said that God "made him to be sin" for our sake, a very dramatic claim that probably reflects the old sacrificial system whereby the victim was thought to carry away the sins of those for whom the sacrifice was offered. However we understand these texts, there can be no doubt that the Christian Church has, from the very beginning, held three things in a mysteriously creative tension. It has believed that Christ was without sin, while feeling the full impact of temptation, and that he was the victim of sin, a chosen sacrifice, whose suffering was on our behalf. All these notes are gathered into a single chord as we contemplate the third station of the cross, where Jesus falls under the heavy burden of the cross.

There seem to have been at least two types of cross used by the Romans in crucifixions. It took either the form T, the *crux commissa,* or the form †, the *crux immissa.* In either case, the victim usually carried the cross beam, the *patibulum,* to the place of execution, often roped to his shoulders. The gospels do not describe the falls of Jesus under the weight of the *patibulum,* though we are told that Simon of Cyrene was dragged out of the crowd to help him carry it, strong evidence that in his weakened state Jesus was taking too long to reach Calvary. In the Stations of the Cross we are called upon three times to meditate upon Jesus falling to the ground.

The most obvious way in which to understand these incidents is on the level of physical weakness. Crucifixion was a hideous form of execution. By its very nature it was, and was meant to be, a slow process. It was death by torture, but the prelude to crucifixion was almost worse. This was the infamous scourging. The victim, stripped to the waist, was either roped to a pillar or stretched out on a frame, and his back was torn to shreds by a whip laced with bone and pieces of metal. Many lost consciousness under the lash; many were driven mad by it. It was a fearsome punishment in its own right, but it was always the prelude to crucifixion. The prisoner, his shoulders and back raw, shredded to the bones beneath, was then roped to a rough and heavy beam of wood and made to bear it to the place of execution. The journey must have seemed endless, made through waves of pain, as the prisoner slipped in and out of consciousness, his lungs bursting, his head drumming with agony. The peculiar anguish of the way of the cross lies in the knowledge that the pain Jesus endured as he staggered up the hill towards Calvary could only be succeeded by greater pain and "grief, pitched past pitch of grief". The distance between the place of sentence and the place of execution was not like the last few miles of a marathon when the runner knows the thing will be over soon and the pain will cease. Jesus went on from pain to pain, filled with the knowledge that greater agony waited for him at the top of the hill. He found the will to go on to the bitterest of ends, but there were times when he collapsed on the way, falling to his knees, on his face, spread-eagled under the weight of his own gallows.

So the obvious way to understand the fall of Jesus is to stress the colossal and weakening punishment he had undergone. His falling is a straightforward consequence of his physical weakness. If we can bear to dwell on it, contemplating the physical torture Jesus underwent may embolden us to endure the pains, great and small, that our own nature has to undergo. There is no life free of pain, and most men and women find it hard to bear. Some have found help in bearing it in the contemplation of the fallen Jesus, struggling to rise from the street, pushing up on to his knees, trying to stand, with his arms roped like a scarecrow to the beam that lies across his shoulders. That is pain enough to contemplate and it may help us to bear the pains of our own flesh, but there are deeper pains than that, and falls more severe. The word "fall" resonates for Christians with numerous echoes, some of them from our own life and its failures, some of them going back to a time beyond time. The word "fall" irresistibly summons the whole Christian tradition of man's first disobedience before us, it brings us face to face with the mystery of Sin.

It is often said that the only Christian doctrine for which there is any empirical evidence is the doctrine of the Fall. The claim is too epigrammatic to be entirely true, but there is much truth in it. It may not be obvious that men and women are destined to eternal life in heaven, but it is perfectly obvious that moral failure characterizes much of their lives on earth. The American historian, Barbara Tuchman, has recently written a book called *The March of Folly,* which sets out to explore certain epochs in human history that demonstrate the almost invincible irrationality of human nature. Her book has an admonitory function, seeking to warn us against further folly, but it is almost certain that it will go unheeded, because it is in our nature to be strangely heedless of even what we know to be in our own best interests. The historian Gibbon was probably closer to the melancholy truth when he wrote that history is "little more than the register of the crimes, follies and misfortunes of mankind''. There is something intractable about human nature. There is in each of us some element of stubborn irrationality that complicates and often completely destroys our search for peace and harmony, at both the private and the corporate level. But the Christian doctrine of the Fall is really only descriptive of this situation; it offers little in the way of explanation.

The Fall is a fact and we must learn to reckon with it, but we are not really told why it happened. It is often thought that the story of the disobedience of Adam and Eve gave rise to the theory of the Fall, but it would be just as true to say that it was the fact of the Fall that gave rise to the story of Adam and Eve. Whether we interpret our first parents' story literally or figuratively, it really does not clear up the mystery of human sinfulness, it merely describes it. Even so, it does it in a way that contains most of the elements of the human predicament. Adam and Eve are representative characters, they are Man and Woman, they are human nature. And their story is the story of happiness lost, of innocence squandered. They stand for that strange impulse in all of us to destroy our own peace by yielding to temptations that offer immediate pleasure, but which cheat us in the long run, by making the achievement of really worthwhile objectives more difficult. But the thing is more profound than that. It is not just about our inability to deny ourselves that guilty visit to the refrigerator or the tobacco shop or the off-licence. These are themselves simply parables of a much deeper impulse in us. There is something in us that desires to kill the thing it loves. There is a profound and constitutional irrationality in us that is at the root of all human misery and could lead to our own destruction as a species. The rejection by Adam and Eve of their own innocent contentment is the sign of all human discontent and irrationality, and it seems to have three characteristics, all present in the story of the Fall of Adam.

We are told in the book of Genesis that the Lord God placed Adam and Eve in a garden, in a state of innocent contentment, but with one limitation upon their freedom: they were not to eat of the Tree of the Knowledge of Good and Evil that stood in the midst of the garden (Genesis 2:15-17). And it is this very limitation, this frontier or boundary, that becomes the unbearable challenge. It is a theme that has been worked out in tragedy and drama in a million different forms, and at its heart lies this strange inability to rest content with what we have and where we are. But it is not simply a matter of wanting to improve the layout of the garden or increase the size of the apple crop. There is, deep within us, a willingness to risk the loss of everything we have and love, for the sake of some wild attraction, some destructive longing, some loneliness that courts personal disaster. One of the modes of this temptation is sexual. Alan Paton's novel, *Too Late the Phalarope,* describes one of these sexual tragedies, played out against the complicating background of South African apartheid. The great white hero, rugby star, policeman, loving husband, destroys his own happiness and the happiness of his family by embarking on an anguished love affair with a black girl, and pulls upon his own head the tragic consequences of adultery. The sexual tragedy is a particularly potent example of the human tendency to self-destruction, for it calls forth from society all the hypocritical passion of outraged self-righteousness. The calm and privacy of many a man who has concealed his anguish behind a mask of respectability has often been blown away by a single injudicious gesture, some furtive and lonely act of passion performed in secret and subsequently proclaimed from the house tops by avid journalists.

Yet it need not be as dramatic or as public as that. In *The Ballad of Reading Gaol,* Oscar Wilde, who knew what he was talking about, warned us:

> Yet each man kills the thing he loves,
>   By each let this be heard,
> Some do it with a bitter look,
>   Some with a flattering word.
> The coward does it with a kiss,
>   The brave man with a sword!

I once saw a film in which the hero complained about his disordered life and his failure to do anything about it: "I keep getting in my own way", he said. We usually know the good we should do, the evil we should avoid, and we know the consequences of our actions and omissions, yet each of us kills the thing he loves. Something in us wants to destroy the walls that are our only protection, though we see all around us the consequences of such irrationality. "History never repeats itself, man always does", said Voltaire, and the clue to our invincible failure to learn from our own history may lie in a profound self-delusion. The parallel is with that strange unspoken conviction we all have, certainly when we are young, that we will never die. Others die all around us, but we shall be exempt. The difficulty we have in envisaging our own death is very like the difficulty we face in the moral sphere: somehow, we persuade ourselves, we shall avoid the consequences of our actions, we shall get away with it, no one will ever find *us* out. Psychologists would call this "narcissism", a profound self-love that blinds us to our real condition. Whatever we call it, it seems to be an inescapable part of our nature.

The second element in the story of Adam and Eve is the ancient human tendency to lay the blame elsewhere. "The woman gave me fruit of the tree and I ate", said Adam. "The serpent beguiled me, and I ate," said Eve. Passing the blame on to someone else is as insistent a characteristic of men and women as is sinning. Our first experience of this sort of scapegoating is usually local and inter-personal. Even rape victims are often accused of provoking their attackers to violate them, but we all do it in ways great and small, and have been doing it since the nursery. "She did it", "He pushed me", "It was his idea," "The woman gave me and I did eat", "The serpent beguiled me." The most immediate motive for this sort of transfer of blame is self-protective. We want to preserve ourselves from attack, so we pull some innocent bystander in front of us and hide behind her. Again, it is evidence of that profound narcissism that afflicts us: the self must be protected at all costs, at the expense of the truth, at the expense of another's life or reputation. Of course, we do not take ourselves in by this ruse, even if we persuade others. That is why we usually end up by hating our victims and attributing all sorts of defects to them that serve as some kind of justification for our own monstrous conduct towards them. The most obvious and immediate type of scapegoating is inter-personal, but history is full of examples where whole peoples and races have been used thus. The tragic history of the Jews is the most glaring example of this desire to seek a victim on whom to visit one's own sins, but other examples abound. They are usually racial minorities, convenient targets for outrage, like the Christians in ancient Rome who were attacked by the mob and blamed for the fire that destroyed the city.

The most complete development of this tendency is the fully elaborated conspiracy theory, usually political, to account for the miseries and inequalities of history. "An enemy hath done this", we cry, as we contemplate the complicated tragedies of time, and the enemies are manifold. If racial scapegoating is usually the work of the mob, venting its frustration and envy on mysterious strangers, then political conspiracy theories are usually the work of lonely intellectuals, wrestling with the intractable elements of human history, and seeking to impose a pattern upon them. Sir Karl Popper called these theoreticians enemies of the open society, because they wished to close and control the frontiers of human behaviour. Their motives are usually high and idealistic—they are persuaded that they have discovered the root of human misery and social disorder. Their operating principle may be eugenic, involving massive interference with whole races and peoples, banning one tribe and exalting another, relocating some groups, exterminating others. Or the principle may be derived from an obsessive investigation of economic activity, leading to whole theories of history and cultural development, almost mystical in their conviction, and involving massive intervention in the private and corporate activities of ordinary men and women. An enemy hath wrought the misery of mankind and the Plan will overthrow the enemy, if it is meticulously carried out.

Our century, perhaps the grimmest in the history of

humanity, has afforded us plenty of examples of the evil men do when they have persuaded themselves that they know the cause of and have the cure for human wickedness. The irony is almost too painful to contemplate, but it is undoubtedly the case that more pain has been inflicted on men and women by those who have claimed to be eradicating pain from history, than by all the accidental pains that flesh is heir to.

The story of Adam and Eve and the forbidden apple contains the two key elements of human sinfulness: the first is a perverse and self-destructive irrationality that courts and frequently precipitates personal and social catastrophe; and the second characteristic, in whatever form it comes, is an instinctive urge to locate the blame elsewhere than in the self, and this projection and displacement of guilt leads to horrifying consequences on every level of human life. We destroy our own happiness and lay the blame on another: "An enemy hath done this." But who is the enemy?

The third and most mysterious element in the story of the Fall is the presence of the serpent. He is the tempter, but where does he come from? Another way to phrase the question would be to accept the description I have given of the human predisposition to sin and to ask whence it came. I have already pointed out that the Christian doctrine of the Fall is essentially descriptive: by means of a story it describes the mysterious human experience of sin, but it does not really offer an explanation. Is any explanation possible?

The three great monotheistic religions, Judaism, Christianity and Islam, do not offer a logical or naturalistic explanation. They assert, instead, that the explanation is supernatural. Whatever the language we use, the assertion implies that there is a form of intelligence in the universe other than our own, and that it has rebelled against its creator. Some thinkers have talked about a pre-cosmic fall to account for the flawed nature of our world: before our universe evolved, some conflict erupted among created, non-material intelligences. It is, of course, very difficult for our minds to grasp this sort of hypothesis, but there is no logical reason why ours should be the only form or order of intelligence in the universe. There are ancient traditions of gradations of being between our own and God's. If it is helpful to think of them as discarnate intelligences, minds without bodies, angelic beings, then it is perfectly logical to do so. The philosopher Mortimer Adler has recently claimed that the existence of angels can be logically demonstrated. They are forms of extra-cosmic intelligence, he claims.

But however we conceptualize it, we are forced back upon some notion of conflict in the realm of created but non-material intelligence, some great struggle at the very threshold of creation. "There was war in heaven", said the strange visionary who wrote the book of Revelation, some rebellion in the very citadel of God. These are not demonstrable claims, of course, but they are not unreasonable and they do offer some sort of explanation of the human predicament. "It feels like a war", said William James, of the strange moral and spiritual conflicts we wage with ourselves, tempted against our own true interests, drawn to the very brink of self-destructive madness by some pressure of evil, some power of darkness that simply hates the light and would draw us away from it. "We are not contending against flesh and blood, but against the principalities, against the powers, against the world rulers of this present darkness, against the spiritual hosts of wickedness in the heavenly places", said Paul (Ephesians 6:12). What we confront is supernatural evil, a force of wickedness in the universe that is pitted against the force of good. In his study of Paul's letter to the Ephesians, Bishop Gore says that rebellion had been in the universe before man. "There are invisible rebel spirits, of whose real existence and influence St Paul had no more doubt than any other Jew who was not a Sadducee. And, indeed, our Lord had so spoken of good and evil spirits as to assure His disciples of their existence and influence. These rebel wills are unseen by us and in most respects unknown, but they organize and give a certain coherence and continuity to evil in the world. There thus arises a sort of kingdom of evil over against the kingdom of God, and those who will not surrender themselves to God and His kingdom, become perforce servants of Satan and his kingdom" (Gore, *Epistle to the Ephesians,* p. 93). Only a claim as grim and sweeping as that can account for all the manifestations of evil, from the incessant struggles of the private conscience right up to the hideously orchestrated and industrialized obscenities of the Third Reich. There is a war on, and it will be waged to the end of time.

There is a war on, and the passion of Christ reflects and represents that war in a variety of ways. It is obviously an incident in that war, another example of the triumph of organized evil over the lonely, good man. But there is more to this event than meets the eye; more is going on here than the human protagonists recognize. Christ falls on this field of battle again and again; as the world sees it, defeat is piled on defeat, but this is because the world sees everything upside down and the wrong way round. We have inverted value, so that the passing riches and fading pleasures of this world, the passions of the outer man, become our chief end. But they are fools' gold, mirages in the desert. They do not abide, and even in this life they cheat us of the pleasure they promise, but they cheat us in an even more profound way. They are only symbols and parables of the enduring joy we were meant to know. Something of the unfading glory of God comes through them, but it is never found in them. That is why the joys of this life are so bewitching and so heart-breaking. They remind us of something we were born remembering and spend our lives forgetting. The kingdom that is at enmity with God and which so easily captures our allegiance is a perverse reflection of our true homeland. All our values and longings are back to front; they deceive us as we clutch them. In Christ, however, we find reality re-established. He re-asserts the real and enduring order, but we only see as the world sees. What God sees as glory we see as abject humiliation. What we see as a falling in the dust is in fact a rising up and a standing against every power that ranges against God. Christ falls, but only to lift us up.

Questions for Discussion

1. What is meant by original sin?

2. How do you explain the existence of sin?

3. Discuss the meaning of supernatural evil.

5
Christ Meets the Women of Jerusalem

The Jewish historian, Josephus, described crucifixion as "the most wretched of all ways of dying", and Marcus Tullius Cicero, the famous Roman orator and politician, said of it: "Even the mere word, cross, must remain far not only from the lips of the citizens of Rome, but also from their thoughts, their eyes, their ears." And elsewhere he called it the grossest, cruelest and most hideous manner of execution known to man. Part of the horror of crucifixion lay in its public nature. It was a spectacle designed partly to entertain, but mainly to intimidate the public. The logic of the deterrent value of crucifixion was followed ruthlessly by parading its victims through the busiest streets of the town. Along his way of sorrows, according to the tradition of the stations of the cross, Jesus had four encounters, two of them described in the gospels, one of them implied and the other almost certainly a pious legend.

Mark tells us that "they compelled a passer-by, Simon of Cyrene, who was coming in from the country, the father of Alexander and Rufus, to carry his cross" (Mark 15:21). Mark gives his full name to distinguish him from other Simons in the gospel story, and he mentions his two sons, as though they were well known to his readers. At the end of his letter to the Romans Paul says, "Greet Rufus, eminent in the Lord" (Romans 16:13). William L. Lane cites an interesting find by Israeli archaeologists in the Kidron Valley in November 1941: a burial-cave used in the first century before the destruction of the Temple and belonging to a family of Cyrenian Jews. "The intriguing possibility that this tomb was owned by Simon and his family is raised by an ossuary inscribed twice in Greek, 'Alexander, son of Simon', although the similarity to Mark's record may be coincidental" (*The Gospel of Mark,* p. 536). Simon, Alexander and Rufus were all common names among the Jews, and we cannot be certain of any of these connections, but we can be quite sure that Rufus and Alexander, the sons of Simon, were Christians, probably living in Rome by the time Mark wrote his gospel, since they are clearly known to his readers. Was Simon already a follower of Jesus when he was plucked out of the crowd by the Roman soldiers? Mark calls him a "passer-by", implying that he was not previously known to Jesus. If we could get behind this tantalizing footnote in the first gospel we might find that Simon and his sons became Christians as a result of that tragic encounter in the streets of Jerusalem. There are many ways to meet Christ and more ways to serve him, for some serve him who do not know him, meeting him incognito in the poor and the suffering. And some meet him because, like Simon, they come across someone in need, stop what they are doing, pick up his cross and carry it for a mile.

According to legend, a woman in the crowd offered her head-cloth to Jesus so that he could wipe the blood and sweat from his face. When he returned it to her his features were impressed upon it, and this relic was greatly venerated in the Middle Ages. It was transferred to St Peter's in Rome in 1297, though other cities also claimed possession of it. According to *The Acts of Pilate,* an apocryphal work, probably dating from the fourth century, a woman named Veronica is supposed to have cured the Emperor Tiberius with a miraculous portrait of Christ, the woman being the one "with an issue of blood" (Matthew 9:20), who sought to touch Jesus and be cured. One medieval account of the legend applies the name Veronica to the cloth as *vera eikōn* ("true image"), while another claims that it was only so named after the woman who possessed it. We need not give much credence to the details of the legend, though the encounter itself is entirely credible. Women played a much nobler role in the passion of Christ than did men, and it is entirely appropriate that this should be symbolized in the sixth station of the cross. In fact, women feature significantly in four stations, including the legend of Veronica. Mary, the mother of Jesus, meets him at the fourth station, and receives his dead body into her arms at the thirteenth. The pietà, a representation of Our Lady lamenting over the dead body of her son, is one of the most moving elements in Christian art, and we shall think about it later in this book. Meanwhile, let me turn to the eighth station, where Jesus meets the women of Jerusalem.

According to Luke, who is always very interested in women and their devotion to Jesus, as Jesus made his way to the place of execution, "There followed him a great multitude of the people, and of women who bewailed and lamented him. But Jesus turning to them said, 'Daughters of Jerusalem, do not weep for me, but weep for yourselves and for your children' " (Luke 23:27-28). Luke is particularly interested in the compassion of Jesus towards the poor, the outcast, and his sympathy and openness towards women. John, too, develops the same theme. He gives us the encounter between Jesus and the

Samaritan woman at Jacob's well in the city of Sychar, an encounter that clearly puzzled his disciples. And it is John who names the brave women who follow Christ to Calvary and stand round the cross till he dies. The loyalty of women to Jesus was clearly the result of the direct appeal he made to them, an appeal that probably contributed to the murderous anger the religious leaders of Jerusalem felt for him. The fact that Jesus addressed women in public and made a quite definite approach to them was extraordinary. It was a precept of the moralists of the time that "a man should not salute a woman in a public place, not even his wife". There was, at the time, a very real contempt for women, though it was doubtless modified in many cases by the genuine love that existed between them and their husbands and sons. Nevertheless, one of the thanksgivings used in the daily service in the Synagogue said: "Blessed art thou, O Lord . . . who hast not made me a woman." This contempt for women was fairly universal. Among pagans, as often as not, a female child would be exposed and left to die immediately after birth, being prized less highly than a son. Though Jews were more tender in their treatment of women, women had few rights among them and could, for instance, be divorced by their husbands on the most frivolous grounds. In this context, therefore, Christ's attitude of openness and directness to women is quite amazing. As we have already seen, he brought a freshness and freedom to his teaching about God and to his relations with men and women that was quite astounding, and clearly contributed to his murder. It is a mistake, of course, to fall into the trap of externalizing the judgements of Jesus, to transfer them to others and never to ourselves. The New Testament is not meant to be an historical source book; it is a mirror to our times; its revelatory power is meant to challenge and disturb our prejudices and attitudes, not to impart a warm glow to us because, unlike those ancient Jews, we are wonderfully free of all the attitudes Jesus denounced.

The words of Jesus to the women of Jerusalem were painfully predictive. Women still weep for themselves and for their children, because they are still the victims of conscious and unconscious discrimination. In some places this discrimination has been practised quite openly for centuries. Statistics cannot measure everything, of course, but they do reflect some part of what is going on in society, and the statistics of discrimination against women are quite interesting. They tell us, for instance, that they comprise more than a third of the world's economically active population. Forty-six out of every hundred women of working age (15-64) are in the labour force, though they earn significantly less than men for the same work, and in some places are virtually used as slaves. In Africa, for instance, 75 per cent of the agricultural work of the continent is carried out by women, often with babies strapped to their backs. Their inferior status throughout the world is underlined by the figures for illiteracy. In the world 28 per cent of the men are illiterate compared to 40.3 per cent of the women. Behind the facts and figures lie a series of ancient and intractable realities. Some of them are stubbornly empirical, such as the obvious limitations that childbearing imposes upon women, especially in primitive societies, and the superior physical strength of men. But many of the attitudes we adopt to what are now called "women's issues" seem to have their origin in the collective unconscious of the race. Only this can account for the desperation and passion that is brought to the current debate about women's ordination, for instance. A similar passion on both sides was brought to bear on the struggle for the vote for women, and deeply entrenched positions were adopted by all the protagonists. One ought to bring to these historic shifts in consciousness an enormous compassion for both sides, and a recognition that people are often only vehicles for the ideas they express. They can be taken captive by a new idea and possessed by it to the exclusion of everything else, or they can be held equally fast by an ancient attitude whose destruction would violate their whole self-understanding. History throws up these great collisions of value from time to time, and out of the conflict new directions are discovered, often after the sort of bitter pain that can be likened to birth-pangs. The role of women in the Church is just such an issue, with many people fearing that it could blow the Church apart. What are the main elements in the conflict?

I think one ought to begin, as far as men are concerned, by pointing out that there are a number of mysterious, often unconscious, factors at work in male attitudes to women; there are a number of matters that are hardly ever mentioned in conversation, but that lurk in the background, influencing and colouring the point of view expressed. To be absolutely blunt about it, one of the things that men find both mysterious and faintly repellent about the female sex is menstruation. This uneasiness goes back a very long time. For instance, the man of the Old Testament was taught that a menstrual woman was ceremonially unclean; this purely biological function was held to render a woman unfit for certain religious acts, and she became a focus of ceremonial infection, so that anyone who touched anything she sat upon was immediately unclean.

When a woman has a discharge of blood which is her regular discharge from her body, she shall be in her impurity for seven days, and whoever touches her shall be unclean until the evening. And everything upon which she lies during her impurity shall be unclean; everything also upon which she sits shall be unclean. And whoever touches her bed shall wash his clothes, and bathe himself in water, and be unclean until the evening. And whoever touches anything upon which she sits shall wash his clothes, and bathe himself in water, and be unclean until the evening; whether it is the bed or anything upon which she sits, when he touches it he shall be unclean until the evening. And if any man lies with her, and her impurity is on him, he shall be unclean seven days; and every bed on which he lies shall be unclean.

If a woman has a discharge of blood for many days, not at the time of her impurity, or if she has a discharge beyond the time of her impurity, all the days of the discharge she shall continue in uncleanness; as in the days of her impurity, she shall be unclean. Every bed on which she lies, all the days of her discharge, shall be to her as the bed of her impurity; and everything on which she sits shall be unclean, as in the uncleanness of her impurity. And whoever touches these things shall be unclean, and shall wash his clothes, and bathe himself in water, and be unclean until the evening. But if she is cleansed of her discharge, she shall count for herself seven days, and after that she shall be clean. And on the eighth day she shall take two turtledoves or two young pigeons, and bring them to the priest, to the door of the tent of meeting. And the priest shall offer one for a sin offering and the other for a burnt offering; and the priest shall make atonement for her before the Lord for her unclean discharge.

(Leviticus 15:19-30)

It will be immediately obvious from this passage that the woman in the crowd who suffered from a haemorrhage and who came up and touched the garment of Jesus had been in a state of ceremonial impurity for twelve years (Matthew 9:20). By being in that crowd she broke the law, and by touching Jesus she rendered him unclean—a fact that did not seem to bother him. This attitude may be far-fetched and far-away, but there is little doubt that there is still something of it around, buried deeply within our consciousness. There are certain churches, for instance, where women are not allowed to enter the sanctuary, because there is felt to be something faintly amiss with them by virtue of their gender. So, behind the things that are said in the debate about women in the Church there may lurk this ancient lingering sense that there is something mysteriously suspect about them that renders them unfit for certain kinds of ceremonial activity.

Another element in the traditional male distrust of, and fascination with, women is their seductive power. In the book of Genesis it is Eve who tempts Adam to eat of the forbidden fruit. Behind this myth lies the male experience of women as fascinating creatures who exert an uncanny influence upon men, seducing them from their commitments and loyalties. This ancient and largely unconscious male perception influences history in all sorts of ways.

For instance, it is one of the most common themes in the novels of William Faulkner. There can be little doubt that this inescapable but uneasy fascination that most men feel for women has undoubtedly influenced and compromised the role of women in most religions. An interesting variation on this theme is provided by the fully-fledged misogynist whose discomfort around women often conceals real hatred.

A more straightforward limitation upon the role of women is the simple fact that they bear children and, until very recently, bore most of the burden of rearing them till they were old enough to fend for themselves. This effectively bound the woman to a very circumscribed role, and still does to a very great extent, though in the West that pattern has been radically modified by planned parenthood and the greater involvement of fathers in the nurture of their children.

If we no longer accept the Levitical code, which condemns a woman to spend a large part of her life in ceremonial uncleanness; and if we recognize honestly, in the words of the old song, that it has always taken two to tango; and if the burden of child-rearing is now shared more equally between husband and wife, at least in certain circles, we have clearly moved into a situation where the role of women in Church and Society will inevitably undergo radical changes, and the debate over the ordination of women to the priesthood is an aspect of that shift in consciousness.

But this is not a suitable place for a discussion on the technical question of women's ordination. History will resolve that issue as it has resolved other, equally contentious matters. What I think we ought to celebrate is the undoubted fact that, in a fundamental sense,

women have had a priesthood that has enriched and
irradiated the Church since they stood in the streets of
Jerusalem and wept over the agony of Christ. By priesthood in this sense I mean the power to mediate something
of the dazzling and inexhaustible reality of God. There
have always been certain attributes of God, aspects of
the divine nature, which, in the main, women have
witnessed to and mediated far better than men, and for
a very good reason. The biblical revelation tells us that
humanity is made in God's image. Humanity is male and
female, so it follows that we reflect in our bi-fold way
something that is united in the nature of God. We can
call this the Male and Female principle in the Godhead.
Jungians talk about the *Animus* and *Anima* in the nature
of every human being. Orientals talk about Yin and Yang.
In biblical categories we would talk about the Fatherhood
and the Motherhood of God. The grief of the women of
Jerusalem reflects something of the anguish of God, like
Rachel weeping for her children. In spite of the politics
of the sex war there has never been a time when these
conjoined insights into the nature of God have not, in fact,
been affirmed and celebrated. One of the historic ways
in which this has been done in Catholic Christianity has
been in devotion to Our Lady, a devotion that has
sometimes approached the deification of the Blessed
Mother. Whatever we may think of the theological
excesses to which this has given rise, it does demonstrate
an ancient human need to affirm the conviction that God
must be, in some important sense, our mother as well
as our father.

Just as important has been the role of women in spiritual
nurture, and in conveying truths about God that male
teachers have laid little stress upon. In my own admittedly

patchy reading on the subject, it seems to me that I have discovered more about the tenderness of God and the patience and long-sufferingness of God in the writings of women than in those of men. To mention only two: Mother Julian of Norwich, who experienced those revelations of divine love in which God nurses and cherishes his children and soothes them with the knowledge that "All will be well and all manner of thing will be well". In spiritual, as opposed to theological, formation, I owe more to Evelyn Underhill than to anyone else. Evelyn was an upper-middle-class English woman, who loved cats and afternoon tea and binding her own books. At the same time she was a mystic and scholar, and a superb guide to other souls struggling towards God. Through her writings there comes a note that is both bracing and gentle, encouraging us towards the great adventure of growing into God. She had a vast influence in her time, beyond that of bishops, priests and deacons by the score, and her writings still help countless souls.

There are numerous others I could mention, as well as millions of unknown women, who taught their children to pray and to love the beauty and lovingkindness of God. That is the priesthood women have always exercised. By it the Church has been preserved from some of the worst excesses of male domination and authority. We should hope and pray that women, in their struggle for what they deem to be equality, will not sacrifice that side of their genius that is more particularly, though not exclusively, theirs. Women are used to standing round the foot of the cross, waiting and watching, weeping for their children. Doubtless they will stand there for some time yet, witnessing to their intense loyalty to Jesus.

Questions for Discussion

1. Why have women been discriminated against in history?

2. Discuss some contemporary examples of discrimination against women in Church and State.

3. What special insights do women bring to our understanding of God?

6
Christ is Nailed to the Cross

When Jesus finally reached the place of execution he was stripped of his garments before being nailed to the cross. All the gospel writers record the keen interest taken by the soldiers in the garments Jesus wore. We are told that they cast lots for his clothing, which suggests that his garments were valuable, worth gambling for. John tells us that the soldiers really only cast lots for his tunic, a long robe, woven without seam, and probably made by the very women who had followed him up to the hill of execution. Finding adequate ways of expressing love can be very difficult for us, and one of the ways in which we do it best is by making something with our own hands for the beloved. The gift becomes a sacrament of our affection, an embodiment of inarticulate love. Wise teachers and leaders understand the language of devotion, so they never spurn such gifts, knowing that they are symbols of love, however inappropriate or embarrassing they might be. In the case of the seamless robe, however, the women who cared for Jesus had clearly produced something that was of value, both for its beauty and for its usefulness. We know he frequently spent whole nights in prayer in lonely places, and the nature of his mission must often have led him far from any decent shelter, so the tunic described in the gospel was probably specifically made to ease the rigours of his ministry. It is a tiny detail, of course, but it does suggest to us that Jesus was probably quite matter-of-fact about such things. His was the asceticism of a will conformed to a particular purpose, not the self-conscious asceticism of one for whom heroic self-denial had become an end in itself. He had work to do, and the work involved endurance and pain, but these were secondary effects of the main purpose, they were not pursued for their own sake.

This is always the principle behind a true and healthy asceticism: in doing the will of God we must learn how to abound and how to be abased. And we will probably learn very quickly that our ordinary lives, lived as far as we can live them in conformity with the spirit of Christ, will afford us many unsought opportunities for stringent self-denial. Herbert Kelly used to say that you could take up your cross and drape yourself elegantly upon it, but it was always someone else who had to hammer the nails in. The Abbé de Caussade coined the phrase, "the sacrament of the present moment", to define the same insight. We find the presence of Christ in our lives by surrendering ourselves to the duties and necessities of our state. Christ is encountered where we are and in what we are doing at this moment, not in some imagined set of ideal circumstances, supposedly more conducive to the spiritual life. This was the lesson Paul learnt in a long and tough life. One did not have to go to extravagant lengths of self-denial in order to discipline and subdue the self; circumstances and the ineluctable pressure of other people supplied all that was needed. Writing to the Philippians from prison in Rome, Paul said: "I have learned, in whatever state I am, to be content. I know how to be abased, and I know how to abound; in any and all circumstances I have learned the secret of facing plenty and hunger, abundance and want. I can do all things in him who strengthens me" (Philippians 4:11). So the seamless robe of Christ suggests many points for meditation. It speaks, first of all, of the devotion and intelligence of the disciples who made it for him. And that act of love for Christ has had many successors. There have always been many people who have found practical ways of serving Christ, though they would never have found the nerve or the vocabulary to put their devotion into words. They probably feel ill at ease at prayer meetings or discussion groups, but they'll rewire the church or cut the grass, give someone a lift to midnight mass or take a collecting can round the neighborhood for Christian Aid. E. M. Forster once sneered at "poor, little talkative Christianity", and one can see what he meant. Fortunately, there have always been thousands of Christians who have talked little and done much, and their patron saints are the anonymous women who got together to weave a seamless robe for the young prophet from Nazareth who often had no place to lay his head.

If they were present on Calvary, they saw that same robe, now terribly stained with blood, being haggled over by the soldiers who were on guard duty at the execution. The Christ who surrendered himself to the love behind the splendid gift of the robe and wore it with uncomplicated gratitude, is now rudely stripped of it, sees it shoved into the kit bag of a Roman soldier, and surrenders himself to its loss. The women who stood by were probably too shocked by the treatment of Christ to waste any time regretting the fate of the robe, but it would have been entirely natural for them to feel the rise of protest in their throats. It is very hard to give up something you have laboured over and loved. The greatest conundrum that faces the Christian disciple is knowing when it is right to defend something precious, something offered to Christ, and when it is right to surrender it, to offer it to Christ in a more profound way by sacrificing it completely. Christ often demands these surrenders from us. We have to give up the beautiful thing we have made for him, and see it handled roughly, perhaps totally destroyed. Down the ages Christians have endured these terrible surrenders of much that they have loved and often they have fought against the surrender in anguish, unable to endure the sight of the rifled nest, the pillaged sanctuary. The Fourth Tempter said it with brutal poignancy to Becket:

> You have also thought, sometimes at your
>   prayers,
> Sometimes hesitating at the angles of stairs,
> And between sleep and waking, early in the
>   morning,
> When the bird cries, have thought of further
>   scorning.
> That nothing lasts, but the wheel turns,
> The nest is rifled, and the bird mourns;
> That the shrine shall be pillaged, and the gold
>   spent,
> The jewels gone for light ladies' ornament,
> The sanctuary broken, and its stores
> Swept into the laps of parasites and whores.
>   (T. S. Eliot, *Murder in the Cathedral*)

Christ loved the seamless robe because it was a thing of beauty, a gift of love, but he surrendered it for the sake of a greater cause. The women in their grief and perplexity surrendered it too, though it was the work of their hands. Our surrenders are rarely easy and unimportant: they are always things we want to cling to, things we know to be precious, but they have to be given up. It seems that the Church has constantly to be giving up its most precious offerings to Christ, perhaps because they can become his rivals. We have to see the sanctuary broken and its stores swept away, again and again, because we are called to "a condition of complete simplicity (costing not less than everything)" (T. S. Eliot, *Little Gidding*).

So far in our contemplation of this stage in the passion of Christ we have thought about the meaning of the seamless robe, and its surrender by Christ who wore it and by those standing near who had woven it. Now we must turn to one of the most painful aspects of the passion, the nakedness of Christ before his enemies and friends on the hill of Calvary. The victims of crucifixion were stripped at the place of execution and exposed to the mockery of the multitude. The secular writers of the period seem to have had a commendable horror of crucifixion, so nowhere are we given a detailed description of the actual procedure. We do know that the victims were crucified naked, though it is possible that on this occasion they wore loincloths in order to cater to Jewish sensitivities. Even that, however, would be only a tiny mitigation of the humiliation intended. To uncover anyone's nakedness was a great offence to Jewish law and sensibility, so the humiliation of Christ must have been acute. Crucifixions were exercises in public pornography, in which every refinement of torture and humiliation was practised. Christ submitted to all of this with no protest, no resistance. He suffered himself to be humiliated, made no attempt to guard his dignity. There was nothing he did not surrender. He had come naked into the world and he allowed them to drive him naked out of it. He clung to nothing, not even to the last shreds of masculine pride. The nakedness of Christ, if we can bring ourselves to think about it, should shatter all our self-importance, all our posturing and striking of attitudes.

That is probably easy to see, though difficult to do. We know that we all hide behind masks and costumes; we all play games with each other, strike attitudes, assume roles. And all that has to go, has to be stripped off. Christ can overcome any defect in us, except pretence. Every sin can be forgiven, except the sin of self-deception, because the self-deceived does not know his need for radical forgiveness. As long as we put up fronts, pretend to be what we are not, then no progress can be made with us. But if we permit the coverings to be stripped away and allow ourselves to be seen in our nakedness and vulnerability, then everything becomes possible again. Miraculously, we discover that no one was taken in by our pretence, that we were loved, when we were loved, in spite of the pose we struck, the person we pretended to be. That is why really radical and honest and searching confession of sin is so liberating. All is admitted, every hidden part is uncovered, nothing lies concealed, and fast upon that stripping and its embarrassment comes for-giveness and acceptance, indeed the coming of grace is coactive with the desperate cry for mercy.

> Betwixt the stirrup and the ground
> Mercy I asked, mercy I found.
> (William Camden)

All of that is painful to do, but it makes sense. What is

much more difficult to accept is the fact that we often have to be stripped of things that are good and precious, we often have to sacrifice the thing or the person we most love. Often we are called upon to abandon, without a backward look, much that we love in the Church and its traditions, for the sake of the will of God. Language and customs that have become hallowed with use may have to be left behind, delivered into the hands of those that would despoil our goods, because there is other work for us to do. We have to suffer it when they cast lots for our vesture. Some are asked to leave family and kindred, to be stripped of all they hold dear, because they are called to go and serve God in some far country. Biblical religion is full of this theme of surrender, of giving up in order to receive, of dying to live. And even if our adventure of faith is lived within the landscape we have always known; even if our surrenders have been within our own mind and heart, and not at all in the drama and bustle of external reality; even then we must accept the necessity of our going hence, of our own dying. One day we must all abandon ourselves to absolute loss.

> Now is the time for stripping the spirit bare,
> Time for the burning of days ended and done,
> Idle solace of things that have gone before:
> Rootless hopes and fruitless desire are there;
> Let them go to the fire, with never a look behind.
> The world that was ours is a world that is ours no
>   more.
>   (Laurence Binyon, *The Burning of the Leaves*)

The stripping of Christ reminds us that we must abandon

the world one day. Life's changes and chances afford us many opportunities for rehearsing that final exit.

After the victim was stripped he was nailed to the cross. As I have already pointed out, the secular writers of the period have nowhere left us with a detailed description of this, the final stage in the sadistic ritual of crucifixion. Interestingly enough, however, certain modern studies and discoveries afford us a very graphic description of what went on. Some of this new information comes to us as a result of studies done on the famous Shroud of Turin. Whatever we may think of that mysterious article, it has stimulated vigorous discussion of what actually happened at a crucifixion. Jerome Goldblatt (*National Review,* 16th April 1982) has reviewed the evidence for the validity of the claim that the Shroud of Turin is the burial cloth in which they wrapped Jesus after his death. He points out that for centuries Christian art has depicted Christ hanging on the cross with nails penetrating the palms of his hands. One of the things that puzzled those who investigated the shroud was the discovery of distinct wrist wounds on the image. Goldblatt tells us that Pierre Barbet, Chief Surgeon of St Joseph's Hospital in Paris in the 'thirties, with access to unclaimed bodies and various amputated limbs, performed some experiments in an attempt to explain the wrist wounds displayed on the shroud's image. He discovered that a nail pounded into the wrist of a freshly amputated arm did not strike a mass of bone, but diverted slightly upward and passed cleanly through. He concluded that this aperture in the wrist must have been known to Roman executioners, who had discovered, as Barbet did centuries later, that bodies hung from nails through the palms tore loose immediately, while those nailed through the wrists would hang securely in place. This rather grisly experiment received confirmation in June 1968 when an ossuary was discovered on Ammunition Hill, north of Jerusalem. It contained the bones of a young man who had plainly been crucified about the beginning of the first century A.D. "One nail had been driven through each of his forearms, and a third, which was still *in situ*, through both his ankles together. His legs had been broken like those of Jesus' two companions in John 19:32" (*Dictionary of New Testament Theology*, Volume 1, p. 393).

However, in the resurrection appearances recorded by John and Luke, Jesus shows his disciples the wounds in his hands and feet. We cannot say confidently, therefore, how the nailing was done, though the Barbet experiment and the discovery on Ammunition Hill do not necessarily contradict the biblical evidence. One possible solution to the tradition that Jesus was nailed through his hands rather than through his wrists would be the presence of a "saddle" on the cross, as is sometimes depicted in Christian art. This would support the weight of the body, which would otherwise tear itself away from the nails through the hands, but it would probably prolong the time spent on the cross. According to Goldblatt's investigation, victims of crucifixion really died of suffocation. He pointed out that when the nails were hammered into the extremities the body was laid out on the cross and the arms would be extended at a ninety-degree angle. However, when the cross was hoisted into an upright position, the victim's arms with the weight of the entire body dragging on them would sag to approximately sixty-five degrees. In that position the muscles would soon start to contract violently. Cramps would spread from the forearms to the upper arms and shoulders before moving into the limbs and trunk. Spasms would cause the fingers and toes to curl inward in a state of tetany. The stomach muscles would tighten to form a hollow beneath the distended rib-cage. The lungs would fill with air, but because of the contraction of the expiratory muscles, they would be unable to expel it and asphyxiation would set in. The only way to stave off death would be to relieve the drag on the hands and arms by using the nail through the feet as a fulcrum, enabling the victim to rise to an upright position. According to Goldblatt this manoeuvre relaxed the effects of tetanization in the muscles and unloaded the air trapped in the lungs, but the effort in making it must have been agonizing. The struggle for air would continue till exhaustion prevented the victim from raising himself upright. Asphyxiation would then follow. If the victims lingered on, the soldiers hastened death by breaking the bones in their legs, thereby preventing them from pushing up for air. John tells us that the two who were crucified with Jesus had their legs broken in this way to hasten their asphyxiation, but when they came to Jesus they found that he was dead already. However, one soldier, in order to leave an official stamp of death upon Jesus, thrust a spear into his side.

Jesus had been on the cross from nine in the morning, according to Mark ("And it was the third hour, when they crucified him", 15:25), until three in the afternoon ("And at the ninth hour . . . Jesus breathed his last", 15:34-37). However, there is some dispute as to the exact hour at which he was crucified, some scholars holding that the note about the third hour was probably added by a scribe to clarify the chronology of the passion. The point is that Christ hung on the cross for no more than six hours before dying. Some victims of crucifixion lingered for days, so Christ's death was something of a surprise to the soldiers who were ordered to finish off the victims some time before the beginning of the weekly Sabbath at six in the evening. But the speed of his passing is not surprising. Scourging alone was enough to kill any man, and we know that Christ was severely scourged. The loss of blood from that fierce whipping, followed by the wounds of the nails, combined with heart-break and fatigue are sufficient to account for his death after only a few hours. At last the ordeal was over. Christ had called his death a cup that he had to drink, a baptism with which he had to be baptized. Now the cup was drained, the baptism accomplished. Before turning to a meditation upon the meaning of this death for Christians, let us try to find out what it meant to Christ.

It is difficult to enter with any confidence into the consciousness of Christ about the meaning of his own life and death. The records we have bear the mark of the experience and contemplation of the first Christians, so we find his life and death to some extent already interpreted for us. We look at Christ through the eyes of those who believed in him, so we see the events they record already influenced by their understanding of his identity. What we have is the testimony of faith. Nevertheless, even if we do look at Christ through the eyes of the first believers, we see something. If we can avoid looking at *them* as they looked at him and, instead, try to look at *him* through their eyes, we can be confident that we do genuinely see and hear him. And there is a strong sense from the gospels that Christ was not simply a helpless victim of evil conspirators, but that he made their murder of him his own act by willingly embracing its inevitability, so that it became, not a tragic accident, but a free act whose effects vastly transcended their squalid purpose. Something of this creative ambiguity is well expressed by Becket in his sermon in *Murder in the Cathedral:* "A martyrdom is never the design of man; for the true martyr is he who has become the instrument of God, who has lost his will in the will of God, not lost it but found it, for he has found freedom in submission to God." This spiritual logic applies supremely to Christ, but it applies everywhere else as well. Apparently meaningless and destructive accidents can be turned into gloriously creative acts by the way they are borne, including our own death. Even that event, of all events the most inevitable, can be something we make our own by the way we approach it. Something Edith Wharton wrote about the death of Henry James captures this very well. She writes:

> His dying was slow and harrowing. The final stroke had been preceded by one or two premonitory ones, each causing a diminution just marked enough for the still conscious intelligence to register it, and the sense of disintegration must have been tragically intensified to a man like James, who had so often and deeply pondered on it, so intently watched for its first symptoms. He is said to have told his old friend Lady Prothero, when she saw him after the first stroke, that in the very act of falling (he was dressing at the time) he heard in the room a voice which was distinctly, it seemed, not his own, saying: "So here it is at last, the distinguished thing!" The phrase is too beautifully characteristic not to be recorded. He saw the distinguished thing coming, faced it, and received it with words worthy of all his dealings with life.
>
> (Edith Wharton, *A Backward Glance*)

We know that Jesus anticipated and embraced his own death. The gospels are full of foreshadowings of it. For instance, when he was asked why his disciples did not fast like the disciples of John the Baptist he replied that they would fast "when the bridegroom is taken away from them" (Mark 2:20). And one of the most stubborn and enduring elements in the tradition is that he taught the disciples that he must suffer many things (Mark 8:31). Mark, who was probably close to the reminiscences of Peter in preparing his gospel, tells us how Peter rebuked Jesus for this gloomy prediction and was severely admonished for so doing. Moreover, the whole tradition of the Last Supper is heavy with anticipation of the death that was to follow. The sharing of the cup was a participation in the shedding of Christ's blood: "This is my blood of the covenant, which is poured out for many" (Mark 14:24). And during the agony in Gethsemane Christ is clearly wrestling with the knowledge of the horror that is about to break upon him: "Abba, Father, all things are possible to thee; remove this cup from me; yet not what I will, but what thou wilt" (Mark 14:36).

None of this is intrinsically unlikely. We know from other episodes in history that men of destiny frequently have premonitions of their own death, and even of the way it will come. The most obvious modern example is Martin Luther King, who was vividly aware of the likelihood that he would die at the hand of an assassin. On the night before he suffered he more or less prophesied his own death on the following day. These men, in fulfilling their destiny, unleash the forces of evil and opposition. Indeed, it probably ought to be said that that is why they are sent to us. They define light in opposition to darkness, and the darkness seeks to overcome them.

It has always been thus. The truly righteous man, as Plato foretold in *The Republic,* will inevitably be crucified, because of the eternal warfare in history between good and evil. The paradox is that it is by their defeats that martyrs truly conquer, for they show to the whole of history that some things are more important than life, and that life cravenly clung to at any cost becomes contemptible. For those, however, who have turned life itself into the supreme and only good, nothing is worth dying for or even fighting for. One thing is as good as another, one value as useful as another, every point of view has something to be said for it, so these martyr figures are really only pursuing some obscure need to destroy themselves. Martyrdom, then, becomes a form of suicide. This is the burden of Richard Brito's speech at the end of *Murder in the Cathedral* when he says of Becket:

> This man, formerly a great public servant, had become a wrecker. Even at the last, he could have given us reason: you have seen how he evaded our questions. And when he had deliberately exasperated us beyond human endurance, he could still have easily escaped; he could have kept himself from us long enough to allow our righteous anger to cool. That was just what he did not wish to happen; he insisted, while we were still inflamed with wrath, that the doors should be opened. Need I say more? I think, with these facts before you, you will unhesitatingly render a verdict of Suicide while of Unsound Mind. It is the only charitable verdict you can give, upon one who was, after all, a great man.

The same could be said of Jesus. He was urged not to go to the feast in Jerusalem because of those who sought to kill him. Even after he had entered the city he could have offered some type of explanation, made some gesture towards accommodation. Instead, he kept silence and went to the cross, but his going was no suicide. He did not encompass his own death, others murdered him. And he did not die because he was tired of life and wished some escape from its intolerable burdens. His death, in fact, was a vivid affirmation of the meaning of life because it demonstrated that it was too important to be lived meanly, clung to cravenly, or purchased at any cost. There was a larger reality than our brief earthly life, and our entrance into that larger reality was somehow premised upon our conduct of this life. If we absolutized the value of earthly life we ran the risk of losing the absolute value of eternal life. A man could save his life and lose his soul. Heart-breakingly beautiful as this life is, it is a thing that shuttles past "swifter than a weaver's beam". It has value, but other values are higher. For instance, Jesus told us that love had a higher value than life, and greater love had no man than this, that a man lay down his life for his friends. The death of Jesus, apparently, was not a despairing act of self-destruction; it was a gift to his friends.

Questions for Discussion

1. Why does God sometimes deprive us of things that are good in themselves?

2. Why is self-deception so deadly and confession so good for the soul?

3. What is the point in contemplating the gory details of the crucifixion?

7
Christ Dies on the Cross

Most people cry at funerals. Death, even the death of the old, is inexpressibly poignant and overwhelms us with a numbing sense of loss. I even cry when I get to the end of biographies and read about the deaths of great men and women whom I have admired but never known. My mind knows that there has to be death and that it has to be distributed randomly, but something in my heart always rebels against it, feels it is not right, ought not to be. We are told that death is the wages of sin, the consequence of the Fall. Behind that mysterious doctrine there lies the recognition that something is amiss with death, and what might have been perceived only as a transition between one stage of development and another is now experienced as inconsolable loss. That is why death fascinates us. It is the last frontier, the final adventure, the plunge that takes us into oblivion and utter forgetfulness or into eternal life and the final perfection that awaits us. Death frightens and fascinates us, and so does the experience of dying. That is why human beings have always been interested in the last words of those they have loved and admired. The dying are further up the line than we are, and maybe they can see something of what is on the other side, what lies ahead, so their final words have a peculiar poignancy. Not all famous last words are prophetic or affecting, however; some are bravely humorous. I love Lord Palmerston's: "Die, my dear doctor? That's the last thing I shall do." Disraeli's last words are even more characteristic. Queen Victoria proposed to visit him as he lay dying and he said: "Why should I see her? She will only want me to give a message to Albert." The most poignant last words must be Beethoven's: "I shall hear in heaven." The two that affect me most come from great Christian leaders. When Father Stephen Sedale lay dying at Kelham, one of his brothers leant over him and asked how he felt: "Excited!" he said. And Bishop Gore's last words, spoken not to anyone but in response to what he saw as he lay dying, were: "Transcendent glory."

All these men died in bed, surrounded by the quiet and comfort that should properly attend a death. Jesus died in very different circumstances. Before he died he summoned up enough energy to commit his mother to the care of the beloved disciple. And we can be fairly certain that in his agony on the cross he was meditating on Psalm 22, an uncannily accurate prophecy of his own dying: "My God, my God, why hast thou forsaken me? Why art thou so far from helping me, from the words of my groaning? . . . I am a worm, and no man; scorned by men, and despised by the people. All who see me mock at me, they make mouths at me, they wag their heads; . . . they have pierced my hands and feet—I can count all my bones —they stare and gloat over me; they divide my garments among them, and for my raiment they cast lots."

But towards the end, vision and consciousness must have been dissolving into snatches of remembrance of times past. They say a man's life is reviewed before his eyes in his last moments. Successive time ceases and a whole lifetime is concentrated, summed up in a moment, in a twinkling of an eye. The life of Jesus had been lived in obedience to the Father. He lived the human story as it should have been lived, in harmony and conformity with the mind of the Father. There was no Fall, no going against the grain of things, no placing of himself in the centre. Instead, there was a radical trust in God that the world percieved as insanity, as turning everything upside down and back to front. That living of life the right way up had been the work he was given to do, the mission he had to accomplish, and because the world had inverted all value and distorted all truth it could not receive him. "He came unto his own and his own received him not", said John. The tragic bias in our nature worked against truth and value, and we cast them out, crying out instead for Barabbas the robber. That is what we did, it is what Jesus Christ came to have us do and the result of it all is our salvation. Was there ever such a paradox as that? So confusing is it, yet so certain is the Church about it, that it spends a large part of its worship and meditation dwelling upon it, searching the mystery of it, dwelling upon the victory won by Christ. Again, we have this fascinating inversion of meaning. No one had been more spectacularly defeated and destroyed than Jesus Christ. All his enemies stood and gloated over the spectacle. Yet their victory was really a defeat, and his defeat was really a victory. Christ himself recognized this through the mist of pain and memory that overwhelmed him towards the end of his long agony. John tells us that his last cry was a shout of accomplishment: *Tetelestai,* it is accomplished; the goal, the end, has been reached. The paradox demands that we keep the strangeness, the otherness of the mystery, intact: we must affirm and understand the bitterness and agony of the death, but we must see it, so to speak, under a certain form of eternity. Both our seeing and our interpreting of what happens have to be transcended, transvaluated, seen from inside, and, as C. S. Lewis said of Christian mysteries, they are bigger on the inside than on the outside.

The death of Christ was a victory, then. But it was not just the triumph of endurance, the victory of courage over pain, though it was certainly that. Something fundamental was altered in the way things are in the universe. A decisive encounter in the struggle against the power of evil was concluded. Somewhere a great wall was breached, a stronghold thrown down, a prison door flung open. The poetry and metaphor are inescapable because the decisiveness of the event seems to be beyond the reach of ordinary discourse. On the face of it, it is an unlikely claim. The world seems to be manifestly unredeemed, in spite of the death of Christ. Certainly, more mystery seems to blow and weave round the doctrine of the Atonement than round any other Christian claim. What kind of meaning can we derive from it? At Easter Christians sing that the cross he endured our salvation hath procured. What does this claim mean? If it means anything, what are we saved from, and how is the salvation effected?

When Maximilian Kolbe, who was recently canonized by the Pope, took the place of the Jewish father in the concentration camp at Auschwitz, he saved him from death. It was a vicarious sacrifice: he died for the other man, so that he might go on living. The Catholic priest saved the Jewish father from death; that is straightforward enough. What is it that Jesus has saved us from? The answer of the New Testament is Sin. Sin is to us what the Nazis and death were to that Jewish parent. But it is still not exactly clear. We know what the Nazis were going to do and we understand the work of Father Kolbe. What is sin doing to us that we need to be rescued from it? The New Testament answers that it is destroying us, killing us spiritually. It is rendering us progressively less and less fit for that bracing life with God, beyond death, that is our final destiny.

> . . . all men, both Jews and Greeks, are under the power of sin, as it is written: "None is righteous, no, not one; no one understands, no one seeks for God. All have turned aside, together they have gone wrong; no one does good, not even one." . . . But while we were yet weak, at the right time Christ died for the ungodly. Why, one will hardly die for a righteous man—though perhaps for a good man one will dare even to die. But God shows his love for us in that while we were yet sinners Christ died for us.
>
> (Romans 3:9-12; 5:6-8)

Now sin and its effects is not a subject that it is fashionable to spend much time on, but it is precisely here that we ought to be careful, in spite of our modern sophistication. Most of us will admit that human beings are very prone to self-deception, even massive self-deception. Three examples might illustrate the point. Most of us know people who have a drink problem, people we love and admire. It is obvious to us and lots of others that they are alcoholics. Alcoholism is a disease that is widely discussed, and its symptoms are widely understood. Characteristically, the alcoholic protects himself against that knowledge, deceives himself, refuses to see what is standing out a mile. As they say in Alcoholics Anonymous, such a person is "into denial".

Let us go back a bit further in time. How did slavetraders manage to go on doing what they did without seeing how evil it was? They were not necessarily any more evil than the general run of humanity, yet they deceived themselves about the presence of a massive source of cruelty and corruption in their lives. And what about the Nazis who herded millions of Jews into the death camps? Were they uniquely wicked? It is more likely that they were practising the ancient art of massive self-deception. Now, if human beings are capable of such obvious and outstanding self-deception, how can we be sure that we are not deceiving ourselves about ourselves in ways both blatant and subtle?

However, there is little point in trying to persuade people about the effects of sin in general terms. The best way to approach the Bible on this subject is to receive it as a personal challenge, to apply it to oneself, even if others think it does not apply to them. According to scripture, sin has created such a serious situation for us that God has had to intervene. John tells us that "God so loved the world that he gave his only Son, that whoever believes in him should not perish but have eternal life. For God sent the Son into the world, not to condemn the world, but that the world might be saved through him" (John 3:16-17). If this is true, if it was sin and its consequences we were rescued from, how was, how is the rescue effected? No final and conclusive answer can be given, but a profound difference has been made by Christ, and it seems to be best defined as making its impact through a series of cumulative influences.

First of all, the presence of Christ has introduced an energy towards good in history that may never actually win unconditionally over evil, but is nevertheless there and holds evil at bay. Examples of goodness, of the triumph of love over hatred and trust over fear, abound. People who try to follow the spirit of Christ are still to be found, if not taking away the sins of the world, then battling against them, modifying their power, neutralizing their effect. If it were possible to take a sort of moral and psychic X-ray of humanity today we would find Christians, millions of them, in all sorts of places quietly and persistently opposing the powers of evil and suffering, quietly holding aloft a small light against the engulfing darkness. We would also find thousands of individuals whose personal struggles against all sorts of destructive behaviour had been strengthened by the power of Christ. We would find people who had been rid of alcoholism, of sexual compulsions, of sheer meaninglessness and loneliness, by means of the presence and example of Christ crucified. It is impossible to systematize this power, to convert it into some kind of automatically potent formula. Nevertheless, certain clear elements seem to be involved, certain fundamental experiences are common to those who turn to Christ and receive him as their saviour. Bishop Gore used to say that we have to understand that three things are going on at the same time in the process of the saving work of Christ.

First of all, we have to think of Jesus in front of us. He sets before us the standard of true humanity. His example builds both longing and shame into us. We are drawn by his moral and spiritual beauty. We are drawn to his purity, his courage and compassion, his strength and authority, his passionate commitment to holiness and obedience. We are drawn towards that pattern of perfection and we feel that it answers our own heart's longings. We are wounded, half-formed creatures and here we see wholeness, sanity, clarity and simplicity. We are drawn by the terrible beauty of Christ, yet at the same time it judges us. So Jesus Christ stands in front of us, filling us with both longing and sorrow.

Then we learn that Jesus is for us. He is on our side. He did not come to condemn us but to save us. He is here for our sake. And this is where the mystery of the cross is at its most powerfully effective. Part of the redemptive strategy of God was to shock us into an awareness of our true condition. In the language used by those who counsel alcoholics, the Incarnation of God in Christ was an intervention, an act of tough love in which Almighty God makes us confront the truth about our condition. And the cross is central to that strategy. Christ takes upon himself all the consequences of human sinfulness in order to show us, to exhibit to us, the real nature of sin. This is what it does! This is where it all ends up! We are familiar with the technique in other fields. We know from all those educational films on the dangers of smoking—which show us in graphic detail what cigarettes do to our lungs— what the consequences of our behaviour are. They exhibit in a dramatic way the results of a certain kind of conduct. The cross, in one sense, is like that. It is an advertisement set up by God to show us the cumulative effect of human sinfulness. And this is where the ancient tradition of sacrifice comes in. All those ancient customs, the offering of crops and animals, even the sacrifice of human beings, were all part of a misty awareness in humanity that sin had to be atoned for and that there was a mysterious law of exchange, whereby the sufferings of one man would one day heal the sins of many. So Christ submits, as a sacrifice, to the consequences of sin, bears them on his body, for us, to wake us up, make us see what has been going on in our lives. He shocks us out of our self-deception. And as the scales fall from our eyes, as the tough love really shows us our true condition, then honesty and contrition begin to sweep through us. Now we know. At last the truth sets us free, and at that point we experience the third aspect of the saving work of Christ.

Jesus is in front of us; Jesus is for us; then Jesus is in us, forgiving us, strengthening us. The central fact is forgiveness. We wake up to our true condition, we repent, and fast upon us comes the forgiveness God has all along been longing to pour upon us. His frustration has been because we cannot be forgiven until we want to be. We cannot receive the gift until we ask for it. That is why the strategy of the cross was so essential: it woke us up to our real condition. Now we can receive the gift. It is, indeed, co-active with our contrition. So Christ in us forgives all that is past and strengthens us to find that amendment of life, that real Christian maturity we seek. As we turn more and more to the Christ within us, his personality permeates ours, his radiance gradually burns through the protective devices we have set up against him and other people, and one day we are free, redeemed, saved by the cross of Christ.

This is one way of sketching the saving power of the cross of Christ. The Church has never defined the doctrine of the Atonement, has never sought to be exact and precise in its accounts of the redemption won by Christ. Instead, it goes on celebrating it in hymn and liturgy, and Christians go on experiencing it in their lives. However, there are certain key elements in it to which we must hold: our salvation is won by an act of sacrificial self-offering by Jesus that shocks us into a true awareness of our condition. This is followed by the healing experience of forgiveness, and the knowledge that Jesus is within us, changing us into his own likeness. And the divine strategy in all this *appeals* to us, though it will never remove the need for us to act, because God never ignores our freedom. Christ hangs there before us, beseeching us to stay and look, and as we gaze upon him, the awful picture of sin's curse becomes at the very same time a shining image of the unconquerable love and mercy of God. That is how the redeeming work is still done today, if only we will stay long enough to see what is really going on.

When I survey the wondrous cross,
On which the Prince of glory died,
My richest gain I count but loss,
And pour contempt on all my pride.

Were the whole realm of nature mine,
That were an offering far too small;
Love so amazing, so divine,
Demands my soul, my life, my all.

Finally, there is a sense in which Christians know that sin has been ultimately defeated by the death of Christ. The power of the cross is not just a matter of its influence on individual souls, although that is of fundamental importance. The mists around this event are thick and baffling, but Christian poetry, Christian spiritual experience, Christian mystical theology have all felt that the death of Christ was a decisive encounter with the powers of evil on a cosmic scale, though we do not yet see its full impact. Somewhere a mighty victory has been won, though it has plunged a spear into the very heart of God. We have already thought about that mysterious phrase in the book of Revelation about "the Lamb that was slain since the foundation of the world". Somehow, God and the Lamb have been waging war against evil since the very foundation of the world, and through the suffering of the sinless one our liberation has been won. We do not yet see it fully disclosed, though we are visited by intimations of it, sudden little rushes of certainty; but one day we shall see it, and seeing it weep that it cost God in Christ so much, and yet rejoice that all sorrow has been turned into joy and that all, at last, has been made well.

Questions for Discussion

1. Why do commentators allege that death is to our era what sex was to the Victorians?

2. What do you mean when you say Christ died to save us from our sins?

3. Can you offer any examples of ways in which this is true in your own experience?

8
The Body of Christ is Placed in the Arms of His Mother

Certain episodes in history are too painful to contemplate except on rare occasions, and neither can the great evils and horrors of history be contemplated in their entirety, but certain events can be taken as archetypes, symbols that convey the nature of the whole sweep of human tragedy. Students of history have their own symbols, their own representative events that summon the sweep and grandeur of human sorrow. It may be the tale of the lynching of a solitary black man by hooded avengers in some stifling southern town. It may be the suicide of a public figure caught by the arc-light of publicity in some pathetic sexual deviation. It may be a representative photograph, a modern pietà from one of the world's endless wars, a weeping woman sitting amidst the rubble in Beirut or Belfast or El Salvador, cradling a dead son in her arms, her mind alive with memories of earlier cradlings of one who filled her heart with love and pride.

The image, the symbol I turn to again and again, when I have the fortitude to face it, comes from the Holocaust. There is a novel that captures it for me, a novel so awful and powerful that I can only turn to it infrequently. It is *The Last of the Just* by André Schwartz-Bart. According to this book, in every generation, in Jewish tradition, thirty-six "just men" are born to take the burden of the world's suffering upon themselves. The book is the story of Ernie Levy, the last of the "just men", who died at

Auschwitz in 1943. At the very end of the story Ernie is in a box-car with some women and children, many of them already dead, lurching towards Auschwitz. It is Ernie's burden to console the inconsolable. The children gather round him for comfort as he cradles in his arms the emaciated corpse of a child who has just died of dysentery, another pietà.

"He was my brother", a little girl said hesitantly, anxiously, as though she had not decided what attitude it would be best to take in front of Ernie.

He sat down next to her and set her on his knees. "He'll wake up too, in a little while, with all the others, when we reach the Kingdom of Israel. There, children can find their parents, and everybody is happy.

"Because the country we're going to, that's our kingdom, you know. There, the sun never sets, and you may eat anything you can think of. There, an eternal joy will crown your heads; cheerfulness and gaiety will come and greet you, and all the pains and all the moans will run away . . ."

"How can you tell them it's only a dream?" one of the women breathed, with hate in her voice. Rocking the child mechanically, Ernie gave way to dry sobs.

"Madame," he said at last, "there is no room for truth here." Then he stopped rocking the child, turned, and saw that the old woman's face had altered.

"Then what is there room for?" she began. And taking a closer look at Ernie, registering all the slightest details of his face, she murmured softly, "Then you don't believe what you're saying at all? Not at all?"

When they reach Auschwitz Ernie leads his little flock of children into the gas chambers: "Breathe deeply, my lambs, and quickly!"

When the layers of gas had covered everything, there was silence in the dark sky of the room for perhaps a minute, broken only by shrill, racking coughs and the gasps of those too far gone in their agonies to offer a devotion. And first as a stream, then a cascade, then an irrepressible, majestic torrent, the poem which, through the smoke of fires and above the funeral pyres of history, the Jews—who for two thousand years never bore arms and never had either missionary empires or coloured slaves—the old love poem which the Jews traced in letters of blood on the earth's hard crust unfurled in the gas chamber, surrounded it, dominated its dark, abysmal sneer: "SHEMA ISRAEL ADONAI ELOHENU ADONAI EH'OTH . . . Hear O Israel, the Eternal our God, the Eternal is One. O Lord by your grace you nourish the living, and by your great pity you resurrect the dead; and you uphold the weak, cure the sick, break the chains of slaves; and faithfully you keep your promises to those who sleep in the dust. Who is like unto you, O merciful Father, and who could be like unto you? . . ."

The voices died one by one along the unfinished poem; the dying children had already dug their nails into Ernie's thighs, and Golda's embrace was already weaker, her kisses were blurred, when suddenly she clung fiercely to her beloved's neck and whispered hoarsely: "Then I'll never see you again? Never again?"

Ernie managed to spit up the needle of fire jabbing at his throat and, as the girl's body slumped against him, its eyes wide in the opaque night, he shouted against her unconscious ear, "In a little while, *I swear it!* . . ."

The book ends:

> At times, it is true, one's heart could break in sorrow. But often too, preferably in the evening, I cannot help thinking that Ernie Levy, dead six million times, is still alive, somewhere, I don't know where . . . Yesterday, as I stood in the street trembling in despair, rooted to the spot, a drop of pity fell from above my face; but there was no breeze in the air, no cloud in the sky . . . there was only a presence.

The only really important question in history is whether the dream Ernie told the children is true. On the way to Auschwitz there was no room for truth, only room for the sustaining, impossible dream. Did Ernie believe it? Do we?

The passion of Christ compels us to ask that question, for it forces us to contemplate the most powerful of all the symbols of human sorrow, the pietà, the cradling of the dead Christ in the arms of his mother. All sorrow is concentrated into that sorrow, all pain is gathered to a single measurable instant. His death represents and foreshadows the interminable dying of time. And what is the truth of that dying? Did he die for an impossible dream? Was he simply broken on the wheel of fate, like all life's victims? Is his death a symbol of all human hopelessness, the archetype of all loss? Did he die in despair like Ernie, waiting for a rescue that never came? Or did he die in hope, knowing that the dream was the truth and all other truth a lie?

No other question is as momentous as that, for upon it hangs the meaning of life. And this is not a question we can suffer others to answer for us, or answer with a formula or a phrase snatched from a creed. This is a question we must answer from within the box-car trundling through the night to Auschwitz, or at the moment we are blindfolded on the gallows, or when we are wheeled into the operating room, or at the moment, "pitched past pitch of grief", when we cradle someone dear above all others now lying dead in our arms, as the universe comes crashing round us. Is the dream true, or is the truth so bleak and empty that we have to fill it with the dream?

Before we try to grapple with the heart of the question, there is something we must note. Grim as it is, a strange paradox remains: the only thing worse than the pain of the universe would be a universe purged of pain. In a universe without pain there would be no pity, and what is more beautiful than pity? The pity, the overwhelming pity of Ernie Levy almost redeems the Holocaust. Only intolerable pain can bring forth intolerable pity, pity raised to such a pitch of love and anguish that it over-whelms the banality of even great evil. Doesn't the pity transcend the pain and bring a terrible beauty from it, though it can never justify it?

In a universe without pain there would be no courage, and what virtue is more splendid than courage? Our history may be tragic, but do we want it stripped of its few heroes who withstood the tyranny of pain, enduring the cross, despising the shame? The universe is ad-mittedly dark and jagged with pain, but do we really want it made safe and bland? Are we really prepared to pay the price of a universe without pain?

The cry of earth's anguish went up unto God,
Lord, take away Pain!
The shadow that darkens the world Thou hast
　　made;
The close coiling chain
That strangles the heart; the burden that weighs
On the wings that would soar.
Lord, take away pain from the world Thou hast
　　made,
That it love Thee the more.

Then answered the Lord to the world He had
　　made,
Shall I take away pain;
And the power of the soul to endure,
Made strong by the strain?
Shall I take away pity, that knits heart to heart,
And sacrifice high?
Will you lose all your heroes that lift from the
　　flame
White brows to the sky?
Shall I take away love that redeems with a price?
And smiles through the loss?
Can ye spare from the lives that would climb unto
　　mine
The Christ on His Cross?

(C.L. Drawbridge)

But even if a universe without pain would be strangely
diminished, there still remains the question: is pain
redeemed or is Ernie's dream only a compassionate lie?
That is a question to which we can never give an irrefut-
able answer. The answer comes by faith, that is to say,

it is wrung out of us, bearing its own validation of meaning or meaninglessness. Real atheists and real believers live by faith, not by demonstration. At the moments faith is summoned from us, Christ, the enigma of history, bears the answer in his own body. We find in Christ a spiritual authority that is simply itself. He does not come to us with references from others, but simply as himself, and he draws from us a response of adoration mingled with doubt, of longing mingled with uncertainty, and that complex is what we call faith. So his authority and strength create the answer of faith in us. But there is something else in him that astonishes us. If his authority, that power in him that compels us to attribute divinity to him, if that draws forth our adoration, our discipleship, then something else in him compels our astonishment, for his divinity is freely conjoined to his sorrow, his suffering; in him we see divinity yoked with abjection. As a consequence sorrow is for ever changed. It is still sorrow—"Ye now therefore have sorrow"—but it is sorrow yoked to a promise. Divinity bears the sorrow, the exceeding sorrowfulness of death, and transmutes it into promise. "You have sorrow now, but I will see you again and your hearts will rejoice, and no one will take your joy from you" (John 16:22). And Christians live by that promise, that dream. They refuse to accept the banality of evil. The passion of Christ has not diminished the evil, but it has for ever altered the way we look at it.

The last two stations are, in many ways, the most poignant of the fourteen. The dead Jesus lying in the arms of his mother is an endless symbol of human sorrow, repeated again and again. The wars of this century have imprinted it upon our memory in a thousand forms. But the symbol of the entombed Jesus, pale and silent in his winding sheet, is just as evocative and, in many ways, more immediately contemporary, because ours seems to be the era of the silent Christ, the inarticulate Christ, the Christ who grips our imagination but who will not explain himself. The helpless Christ seems made for our times, the Christ of the silent tomb. Many of us are puzzled by the complexity of the evils that confront us in the world, and paralysed by our own private frailties. And Christ is often advertised as a miracle worker, as a political and personal messiah. Let him into the situation, some say, whether it be the struggle between nations or the struggle in our lives, and he will bring peace. That's what the disciples wanted, it is what we want and it is what some preach, but it does not seem to be true for everyone. Many of the ones closest to him seem to be the most afflicted. In my own experience, the men and women who have ministered to me the most effectively have been flawed characters, often tragic in their moral frailty, desperate for Christ to deliver them from their fears and compulsions, but their Christ has been the Christ of the silent tomb. He just waits, and so do they. They wait down the years for some lifting of the burden, and it usually does not come. As they say, they learn to live with it. Much of the pain that besets human beings is intractable. Conflicts between nations are tangled skeins of misunderstanding and ancient evil. Herbert Kelly used to say that you could trace the origins of the First World War back to the building of the Great Wall of China. Christ did not offer simple solutions to these ancient complexities, and there seems to be no simple way of applying either his message or his presence. And the same is true of our private histories. Most of us are formed by forces beyond our power to alter, and adding a cubit to our moral stature seems incredibly difficult. Any priest who spends enough time in the confessional learns this, and the knowledge weakens him, softens his desire to judge. Often all that is left is pity, pity for the many ways men and women feel pain, and disappoint themselves.

For many their Christ is the Christ of the tomb, the waiting Christ, the silent Christ. And many of them learn to wait, find an answer in the waiting, and see that the waiting is not an empty thing; it is not an absence of something, it is a more powerful kind of presence. Like Paul whose "thorn in the flesh" was not removed, the waiting is the way they know God, whose strength is made perfect in weakness. After a while they no longer wait impatiently for something to happen, because the waiting is the happening, it is the way they follow Christ, the waiting becomes the way.

> I said to my soul, be still, and wait without hope
> For hope would be hope for the wrong thing;
>   wait without love
> For love would be love of the wrong thing; there
>   is yet faith
> But the faith and the love and the hope are all in
>   the waiting.
> Wait without thought, for you are not ready for
>   thought:
> So the darkness shall be the light, and the
>   stillness the dancing.
>
>   (T.S. Eliot, *East Coker*)

The way of the crucified is the way of joy in sorrow. Christ is the wounded healer, the dying life-giver, the man of sorrows in whom we rejoice. We cannot understand his death and his wait in the tomb. It wrings our heart, compels us to gaze at the unbearable face of evil—a nailed hand, a child's shoe in the middle of the street in the wake of a speeding car, the ditch at Babi Yar, the tokens, the wounds of the Christ crucified until the end of time. And as we listen and gaze, the sorrow not a whit diminished, a wild hope rises in us, something answers from within, and from beyond tragedy, beyond the tomb, beyond hell itself we hear the great promise of the Christ of sorrow and of joy: "Ye now therefore have sorrow, but I will see you again and your hearts will rejoice, and your joy no one will take from you."

Questions for Discussion

1. What effect has the Jewish Holocaust had upon the contemporary understanding of God?

2. What do Christians mean when they talk about the Crucified God?

3. What do we learn from Christ's wait in the tomb?

Epilogue

Resurrection

Some years ago I took part in a rather unsatisfactory debate on television. I had just produced a little book that ran counter to the dominant trend in the religious thought of the time, and I was set up to defend my ideas. In opposition there was a Marxist sociologist and a nuclear physicist, who retained a connection with the Christian Church but who felt that its faith needed to be radically changed. The Marxist said nothing that was not entirely predictable. His main attack was upon the fact that Christians had a bad record for persecuting and destroying each other. My response was simply to say that for a Marxist to oppose Christianity on those grounds was highly ironic. The other man was more difficult to answer. In common with a lot of Christians at the time, he wanted the Church to be stripped of everything that was not concerned with this world. Talk of God and worship and life after death was obsolete. What was needed was to translate the Christian Gospel so that it referred only to this life, which was the only life there was. He was a good example of his own ideas, since he was actively engaged in practising what he preached.

As he spoke I remembered something that had happened to me some years before. I had become rector of a church in Edinburgh in 1968. During my first week I was asked to visit a particular parishioner at her home. I had heard much about her. She was very active in the church, and took a special interest in our nursery school, so I thought it was probably something to do with that. I arrived at her home, and her husband showed me into her room, where she was sitting up in bed. She thanked me for coming and went on: "Now, Father, I've been waiting for your arrival. My doctors have just told me that I am dying of cancer and have, at the most, two months to live. We haven't much time left. Will you, please, prepare me for death and help me to die as a Christian?" And she stopped. I tried to look as if it were the kind of thing I was asked to do every day of the week. I offered a silent prayer for guidance, and then tried to proclaim the Christian Gospel. After that I went to her once or twice a week, and we studied the Bible together, especially the great fifteenth chapter of Paul's First Letter to the Corinthians. As a result, I came closer to an understanding of the Gospel, and she showed me how much further into the heart of it she was than I, who was supposed to be helping her. What emerged was something very simple, but something that is the pure essence of the Christian faith. When you have cleared everything away, when all hope or expectation for this life is utterly removed and there is no longer any human answer, what are you left with? Kitty Hope had reached the very extremity of human hope, she had reached the end of all things. All that awaited her was the great void and abyss of death, the great nothingness that awaits us all, and which we spend much of our life trying not to think of. But she had to think of it: it was the only certain thing that her future held, and each day brought it closer, made it more immediate. The question she wanted answered was this: "Is it simply Nothing that awaits me?" And she did not ask the question with panic or fear or desperation.

She simply asked it: at the end of all ends, stripped down to the solitary self, what awaits us?

The Christian answer to that question, the question which lurks behind our whole life and its meaning, is this: it is not Nothing that awaits us, but the Father, our Father. So while death is a separation, it is also a homecoming. How do we know this, on what do we base this claim? On the Resurrection of Jesus Christ. Paul says that the Resurrection of Jesus Christ is a pledge to us, a guarantee from God, signed and sealed, that, just as he raised Jesus, so he will raise us also and bring us into his presence; and he goes on: "So we do not lose heart. Though our outer nature is wasting away, our inner nature is being renewed every day. For this slight momentary affliction is preparing for us an eternal weight of glory beyond all comparison, because we look not to the things that are seen but to the things that are unseen; for the things that are seen are transient, but the things that are unseen are eternal" (2 Corinthians 4:16-18). The Christian faith does not help us to escape from death, does not sweeten its bitterness, but it assures us that, at the final point of human weakness and defeat, at the moment when we are utterly brought to naught, we meet God and are raised by him. Kitty Hope died six weeks after my first visit to her, and her funeral was one of the best Easter services I have known.

So I asked my nuclear physicist friend how he would have answered the question put by Kitty Hope. He gave no answer, but Paul had given one centuries before: "If for this life only we have hoped in Christ, we are of all men most to be pitied" (1 Corinthians 15:19). But my friend was saying something important, something true, something about the Resurrection. For the Resurrection

is not just a solace as we face death, it is not just a
guarantee that God will be with us at the final End.
The Resurrection is now! In the midst of life we are
in death, day by day we come to all sorts of ends, we
meet defeat and the dying of our hopes, and the Father
meets us there too. In the midst of life we are in the
Resurrection. The Resurrection is now, as well as then;
it is here, as well as there. And this, too, is proof.
We can have confidence that he will be with us at the
end of all ends, because we can experience him in the
midst of the endless endingness that characterizes our
life now. But the process is always the same: we meet
the Father only when we have gone through the dying.
The Resurrection is never an evasion of death, it is
consequent upon death, it only comes when we have
plumbed the depths.

   This is true in our own private struggle with sin. Paul
says that we are to die to sin in order to rise to righteousness. That does not only mean that we are to give up
sin and take up goodness. We are to *die* to sin. What does
it mean to die? It means that we are to accept the
absolutely inescapable, the utterly unavoidable, and go
down into it—we have to face it in its final reality. When
we die to sin, therefore, we are to confront our sin, look
it in the face, recognize it utterly without flinching. We
cannot deal with it any other way: we dare not hide from
it, pretend it is other than it is, run from it, the way we
run from the knowledge of death. We are not to dream
up excuses, or develop ways of explaining it away, or
blame it on someone else. We are to face up to it and
its certainty. Only then, only at that rock-bottom point
of penitence, can we hear the word that raises us to a
new and joyful life. At the very moment of hopelessness,

when we confront, possibly for the first time, what we really are, that very moment is the Resurrection now!

And the same is true in our relationships with each other. Nothing is sadder than broken relationships and the suspicion, hatred and malice that result. And nothing is worse for the Christian or the Christian community than that. But here again, there is to be no superficial healing or patching up. Here, too, we must die, must really face what we have done, what we have become, how we have handled others, abused them, ignored them, exploited them, taken them for granted, taunted and tortured them in ways both blatant and subtle. And what a dying it is to recognize all that: to climb out from behind all our protective fortifications and see the havoc we have wrought; to have our eyes really forced to look long and honestly at what we are, without benefit of that professional advocate who is always there to leap in to our defence and explain it all away. There is no dying like that dying, but there is no substitute for it, no escape from it, if we would have honest and healthy relationships that are not built on pretence or on tyranny. Think of the marriages that are collisions of strangers. Think of the working relationships that are snarling cockpits of hatred and tension. Think of the congregations that are war zones of feuding interest groups, or, which is almost as bad, little bands of friends who freeze out any hapless stranger who inadvertently wanders into their midst. We cannot know the healing of any of these relationships, we cannot live the Resurrection life, until we have faced unflinchingly the reality of what we are. We must die if we would rise again.

And there is another way in which the Resurrection comes, though it often seems to delay its coming. Strange invasions of despair and depression afflict many people today, smothering them in a black cloud of hopelessness and anxiety. Depression is the black plague of our era. No one knows whence it comes, but come it does, welling up from some strange region of lostness, some bleak wasteland of the spirit, to cast a spell upon its luckless victims. It is as much a fact of our time as sin and severed relationships, it is as much a curse as poverty and disease. It is part of the weight that oppresses us and blots out God and his love. It is part of the mystery of iniquity. But here, too, the Resurrection is known. The Resurrection is not just about the reconstitution of the broken body of Christ into an eternal and ineffaceable glory. It is a pledge to us, a sign that God is at work now, restoring his damaged creation to its original pattern. And it is costly work, bloody work, because evil is real and its tentacles range through time. Here, too, we must accept the reality of death, the reality of our situation; we must, somehow, say "yes" to the dying of the light. In the mysterious words of Mother Julian, we are "to be enthusiastic over the Night—and thou shalt see that all manner of things shall be well". And it is the testimony of many, that even here the Resurrection is now, though it creeps upon us unaware. For many it comes in certain passages of music. For others it was a voice they heard "high and soft and from far away like the voice a child hears calling him home, at the end of a long summer dusk". For some, it came in the sight of the first brave flowers of spring on a wild April morning. Come it does, as a lifting and lessening of a burden, a quiet sense of release, a sense that the night is, at last, over and gone. If we wait for it, it will come. It is the experience of the Resurrection now. For the Christian it comes supremely in that strange, broken image of the young Christ setting his face towards Calvary to die there. But another image replaces that one, without completely removing it, so that we see both at once. We continue to see that endless going up to Calvary, and that suffering and that dying. Then there is that hush before dawn in the garden where they laid him. No movement. Only the strange and wistful twilight of yesterday's grave. And then a sudden and terrible glory rises from that ancient sorrow. Suffering itself is transfigured and that dying becomes the Resurrection.

"There *was* a real railway accident", said Aslan softly. "Your father and mother and all of you are—as you used to call it in shadowlands—dead. The term is over; the holidays have begun. The dream is ended: this is the morning."

(C.S. Lewis, *The Last Battle*)

Questions for Discussion

1. What is the meaning of the Resurrection for our lives now?

2. What is the Resurrection Hope?